Linux Containers and Virtualization

Utilizing Rust for Linux Containers

Second Edition

Shashank Mohan Jain

Apress®

Linux Containers and Virtualization: Utilizing Rust for Linux Containers

Shashank Mohan Jain
Bengaluru, India

ISBN-13 (pbk): 978-1-4842-9767-4   ISBN-13 (electronic): 978-1-4842-9768-1
https://doi.org/10.1007/978-1-4842-9768-1

Managing Director, Apress Media LLC: Welmoed Spahr
Acquisitions Editor: Divya Modi
Development Editor: James Markham
Copy Editor: Bill McManus

Cover designed by eStudioCalamar

Cover image designed by Freepik (www.freepik.com)

Distributed to the book trade worldwide by Springer Science+Business Media New York, 1 New York Plaza, Suite 4600, New York, NY 10004-1562, USA. Phone 1-800-SPRINGER, fax (201) 348-4505, e-mail orders-ny@springer-sbm.com, or visit www.springeronline.com. Apress Media, LLC is a California LLC and the sole member (owner) is Springer Science + Business Media Finance Inc (SSBM Finance Inc). SSBM Finance Inc is a **Delaware** corporation.

For information on translations, please e-mail booktranslations@springernature.com; for reprint, paperback, or audio rights, please e-mail bookpermissions@springernature.com.

Apress titles may be purchased in bulk for academic, corporate, or promotional use. eBook versions and licenses are also available for most titles. For more information, reference our Print and eBook Bulk Sales web page at https://www.apress.com/bulk-sales.

Any source code or other supplementary material referenced by the author in this book is available to readers on GitHub (https://github.com/apress). For more detailed information, please visit https://www.apress.com/gp/services/source-code.

Paper in this product is recyclable

Table of Contents

About the Author ix

About the Technical Reviewer xi

Chapter 1: Virtualization Basics 1

History of Virtualization 1

What Is Virtualization? 2

    VM-Based Virtualization 3

    Container-Based Virtualization 3

Hypervisors 4

    Virtual Machine Monitor 4

    Device Model 5

Memory Virtualization 6

    Shadow Page Tables..7

    Nested Page Tables with Hardware Support 7

CPU Virtualization 8

    Binary Translation in the Case of Full Virtualization 9

    Paravirtualization in the Case of XEN with Hypercalls.....................9

IO Virtualization 11

    Full Virtualization 11

    Paravirtualization..11

Summary..14

Chapter 2: Hypervisors 15

The Intel Vt-x Instruction Set...15

The Quick Emulator...19

Creating a VM Using the KVM Module...21

Vhost-Based Data Communication 22

What Is an eventfd? 24

Alternative Virtualization Mechanisms..25

    Unikernels 26

    Project Dune 28

    novm...29

    Summary of Alternative Virtualization Approaches 30

Summary..31

Chapter 3: Namespaces 33

Namespace Types 34

    UTS 35

    PID 35

    Mount 35

    Network...37

    IPC 37

    Cgroup..37

    Time..38

Data Structures for Linux Namespaces 38

Adding a Device to a Namespace 45

Summary..45

Chapter 4: Cgroups 47

Creating a Sample Cgroup 48

Cgroup Types..52

CPU Cgroup...52

Block I/O Cgroups...63

Understanding Fairness...68

Understanding Throttling 71

Summary...81

Chapter 5: Layered File Systems 83

A File System Primer..83

Brief Overview of Pseudo File Systems 87

Understanding layered File Systems..89

The Union File System 90

OverlayFS..90

Summary...93

Chapter 6: Creating a Simple Container Framework 95

The UTS Namespace...95

Golang Installation 97

Building a Container with a Namespace...98

Adding More Namespaces 100

Launching a Shell Program Within the Container 107

Providing the Root File System 110

The Mount Proc File System 116

Enabling the Network for the Container.......................................119

Virtual Networking: A Brief Primer..119

Enabling Cgroups for the Container 134

Summary..143

Chapter 7: Why Choose Rust 145

Introduction..145

Rust Installation 146

Variables 147

Data Types..150

    Primitive Data Types 150

    Compound Data Types 152

Functions 158

    Defining Functions..158

    Calling Functions 159

    Function Arguments 159

    Function Return Values...160

    Function Scope and Lifetime...161

    Function Overloading..161

Generics 162

Conditional Logic 163

    If/Else Statements 163

    Loops...164

    Match Expressions 165

Exception Handling 166

Rust Security Features...169

    Ownership System 170

    Lifetimes...171

    Pattern Matching 173

    Closures..176

    Traits...178

Summary...180

Chapter 8: Containers in Rust...**181**

Refreshing Linux Namespaces?..181

Creating a PID Namespace 182

Creating a Network Namespace 187

Creating a Mount Namespace..191

Writing Complete Container Code 194

Summary...200

Index...**201**

About the Author

Shashank Mohan Jain has been working in the IT industry for more than 20 years, mainly in the areas of cloud computing and distributed systems. He has a keen interest in virtualization techniques, security, and complex systems. Shashank has 39 software patents (many yet to be published) to his name in the area of cloud computing, IoT, and machine learning. He has been a speaker at multiple reputed cloud conferences. Shashank holds Sun, Microsoft, and Linux kernel certifications.

About the Technical Reviewer

Nikhil Jain is an Ansible expert with over 12 years of DevOps experience. He has been using Ansible and contributing to it from its inception. He currently works closely with Ansible Engineering.

He is an open source enthusiast and is part of the Ansible Pune Meetup Organizing team. He has presented multiple Ansible sessions at various global and local events. Apart from sitting in front of his computer automating things using Ansible, he loves watching sports and is a regular part of the local cricket team.

CHAPTER 1

Virtualization Basics

This chapter explains the basics of virtualization, which will be helpful for you to know when you create your own slimmed-down version of a container framework like Docker in subsequent chapters. Before we get into that process, you need to understand how the Linux kernel supports virtualization and how the evolution of the Linux kernel and CPUs has helped advance virtual machines in terms of performance, which in turn led to the creation of containerization technologies.

This chapter also explains what a virtual machine is and what is happening under its hood. We also look into some of the basics of hypervisors, which make it possible to run a virtual machine in a system.

History of Virtualization

Prior to the virtualization era, the only way to provision full physical servers was via IT. This was a costly and time-consuming process. One of the major drawbacks of this method was that the machine's resources— like the CPU, memory, and disks—remained underutilized. To get around this, the notion of *virtualization* started to gain traction.

The history of virtualization goes back to the 1960s, when Jim Rymarczyk, who was a programmer with IBM, started virtualizing the IBM mainframe. IBM designed the CP-40 mainframe for internal usage. This system evolved into the CP-67, which used partition technology to run multiple applications at once. Finally came UNIX, which allowed multiple

© Shashank Mohan Jain 2023
S. M. Jain, *Linux Containers and Virtualization*,
https://doi.org/10.1007/978-1-4842-9768-1_1

programs to run on the x86 hardware. Still, the problem of portability remained. In the early 1990s, Sun Microsystems came up with Java, which allowed the "write once, run anywhere" paradigm to spread its wings. A user could now write a program in Java that could run across a variety of hardware architectures. Java did this by introducing intermediary code (called *bytecode*), which could then be executed on a Java runtime across different hardware architectures. This was the advent of *process-level virtualization,* whereby the Java runtime environment virtualized the POSIX layer.

In the late 1990s, VMware stepped in and launched its own virtualization model. This was related to virtualizing the actual hardware, like the CPU, memory, disks, and so on. This meant that on top of the VMware software (also called the *hypervisor*), we could run operating systems themselves (called *guests*). This in turn meant that developers were not restricted to just running Java programs, but could run any program meant to be run on the guest operating system (OS).

Around 2001, VMware launched the ESX and GSX servers. GSX was a Type 2 hypervisor, meaning it needed an operating system like Windows to run guests. ESX was a Type 1 hypervisor (succeeded by VMware ESXi), which allowed guest OSs to be run directly on the hypervisor.

What Is Virtualization?

Virtualization provides abstraction on top of the actual resources we want to virtualize. The level at which this abstraction is applied changes the way that different virtualization techniques look.

At a higher level, there are two major virtualization techniques based on the level of abstraction:

- Virtual machine (VM) based

- Container based

Apart from these two virtualizing techniques, there are other techniques, such as *unikernels*, which are lightweight, single-purpose VMs. IBM is currently attempting to run unikernels as processes with projects like Nabla. In this book, we will mainly look only at VM-based virtualization and container-based virtualization.

VM-Based Virtualization

The VM-based approach virtualizes the complete OS. The abstraction it presents to the VM is in the form of virtual devices like virtual disks, virtual CPUs, and virtual NICs. In other words, the VM-based approach virtualizes the complete instruction set architecture (ISA); as an example, the x86 ISA.

With virtual machines, multiple OSs can share the same hardware resources, with virtualized representations of each of the resources available to the VM. For example, the OS on the virtual machine (also called the *guest*) can continue to do I/O operations on a disk (in this case, it's a virtual disk), thinking that it's the only OS running on the physical hardware (also called the *host*), although in actuality, it is shared by multiple VMs as well as by the host OS.

VMs are very similar to other processes in the host OS. VMs execute in a hardware-isolated virtual address space and at a lower privilege level than the host OS. The primary difference between a process and a VM is the application binary interface (ABI) exposed by the host to the VM. In the case of a process, the exposed ABI has constructs like network sockets, File Descriptors (FDs), and so on, whereas with full-fledged OS virtualization, the ABI has a virtual disk, a virtual CPU, virtual network cards, and so on.

Container-Based Virtualization

This form of virtualization doesn't abstract the hardware but uses techniques within the Linux kernel to isolate access paths for different resources. It carves out a logical boundary within the same operating system. As an example, container-based virtualization provides a separate root file system, a separate process tree, a separate network subsystem, and so on.

Hypervisors

A special piece of software is used to virtualize the OS, called the *hypervisor*. The hypervisor itself has two parts:

- **Virtual machine monitor (VMM)**: Used for trapping and emulating the privileged instruction set (which only the kernel of the operating system can perform)

- **Device model**: Used for virtualizing the I/O devices

Virtual Machine Monitor

Since the hardware is not available directly on a virtual machine (although in some cases it can be), the VMM traps privileged instructions that access the hardware (like disk/network card) and executes these instructions on behalf of the virtual machine.

The VMM has to satisfy three properties (Popek and Goldberg, 1973):

- **Isolation**: Should isolate guests (VMs) from each other.

- **Equivalency**: Should behave the same with or without virtualization. This means the majority (almost all) of the instructions are run on the physical hardware without any translation, and so on.

- **Performance**: Should perform as good as it does without any virtualization. This again means that the overhead of running a VM is minimal.

Some of the common functionalities of the VMM are as follows:

- Does not allow the VM to access privileged states; that is, things like manipulating the state of certain host registers should not be allowed from the VM. The VMM will always trap and emulate those calls.

- Handles exceptions and interrupts. If a network call (i.e., a request) is issued from within a VM, it will be trapped in the VMM and emulated. On receipt of a response over the physical network/NIC, the CPU will generate an interrupt and deliver it to the actual VM that it's addressed to.

- Handles CPU virtualization by running the majority of the instructions natively (within the virtual CPU of the VM) and only trapping for certain privileged instructions. This means the performance is almost as good as native code running directly on the hardware.

- Handles memory-mapped I/O by mapping the calls to the virtual device–mapped memory in the guest to the actual physical device–mapped memory. For this, the VMM should control the physical memory mappings (guest physical memory to host physical memory). More details are provided later in this chapter.

Device Model

The device model of the hypervisor handles the I/O virtualization again by trapping and emulating and then delivering interrupts back to the specific virtual machine.

Memory Virtualization

One of the critical challenges with virtualization is how to virtualize the memory. The guest OS should have the same behavior as the nonvirtualized OS. This means that the guest OS should probably be at least perceive that it controls the memory.

In the case of virtualization, the guest OS cannot be given direct access to the physical memory. That means the guest OS should not be able to manipulate the hardware page tables, as this can lead to the guest taking control of the physical system.

Before we delve into how this is tackled, a basic understanding of memory virtualization is needed, even in the context of normal OS and hardware interactions.

The OS provides its processes a virtual view of memory; any access to the physical memory is intercepted and handled by the hardware component called the memory management unit (MMU). The OS sets up the CR3 register (via a privileged instruction) and the MMU uses this entry to walk the page tables to determine the physical mapping. The OS also takes care of changing these mappings when allocation and deallocation of physical memory happens.

Now, in the case of virtualized guests, the behavior should be similar. The guest should not get direct access to the physical memory, but should be intercepted and handled by the VMM.

Basically, there are three memory abstractions involved when running a guest OS:

- **Guest virtual memory**: This is what the process running on the guest OS sees.

- **Guest physical memory**: This is what the guest OS sees.

- **System physical memory**: This is what the VMM sees.

There are two possible approaches to handle this:

- Shadow page tables
- Nested page tables with hardware support

Shadow Page Tables

In the case of shadow page tables, the guest virtual memory is mapped directly to the system physical memory via the VMM. This improves performance by avoiding one additional layer of translation. But this approach has a drawback: when there is a change to the guest page tables, the shadow page tables need to be updated. This means there has to be a trap and emulation into the VMM to handle this. The VMM can do this by marking the guest page tables as read-only. That way, any attempt by the guest OS to write to them causes a trap and the VMM can then update the shadow tables.

Nested Page Tables with Hardware Support

Intel and AMD provided a solution to this problem via hardware extensions. Intel provides something called an *Extended Page Table (EPT)*, which allows the MMU to walk two page tables.

The first walk is from the guest virtual memory to the guest physical memory, and the second walk is from the guest physical memory to the system physical memory. Since all this translation now happens in the hardware, there is no need to maintain shadow page tables. Guest page tables are maintained by the guest OS, and the other page table is maintained by the VMM.

With shadow page tables, the translation look-aside buffer (TLB, part of the MMU) cache needs to be flushed on a context switch, that is, bringing up another VM. By contrast, in the case of an extended page table, the hardware introduces a VM identifier via the address space identifier, which means the TLB cache can have mappings for different VMs at the same time, which is a performance boost.

CPU Virtualization

Before we look into CPU virtualization, you should understand the concept of *protection rings* built into the x86 architecture. These rings allow the CPU to protect memory and control privileges and determine what code executes at what privilege level.

The kernel runs in the most privileged mode, Ring 0, and the user space used for running processes runs in Ring 3.

The hardware requires that all privileged instructions be executed in Ring 0. If any attempt is made to run a privileged instruction in Ring 3, the CPU generates a fault. The kernel has registered fault handlers and, based on the fault type, a fault handler is invoked. The corresponding fault handler does a sanity check on the fault and processes it. If a sanity check passes, the fault handler handles the execution on behalf of the process. In the case of VM-based virtualization, the VM is run as a process on the host OS, so if a fault is not handled, the whole VM could be killed.

At a high level, privilege instruction execution from Ring 3 is controlled by a code segment register via the code privilege level (CPL) bit. All calls from Ring 3 are gated to Ring 0. As an example, a system call can be made by an instruction like syscall (from user space), which in turn sets the right CPL level and executes the kernel code with a higher privilege level. Any attempt to directly call high-privilege code from upper rings leads to a hardware fault.

The same concept applies to a virtualized OS. In this case, the guest is deprivileged and runs in Ring 1 and the process of the guest runs in Ring 3. The VMM itself runs in Ring 0. With fully virtualized guests, any privileged instruction has to be trapped and emulated. The VMM emulates the trapped instruction. Over and above the privileged instructions, the sensitive instructions also need to be trapped and emulated by the VMM.

Older versions of x86 CPUs are not virtualizable, which means not all sensitive instructions are privileged. Instructions like SGDT, SIDT, and more can be executed in Ring 1 without being trapped. This can be harmful when running a guest OS, as this could allow the guest to peek at the host kernel data structures. This problem can be addressed in two ways:

- Binary translation in the case of full virtualization

- Paravirtualization in the case of XEN with hypercalls

Binary Translation in the Case of Full Virtualization

In this case, the guest OS is used without any changes. The instructions are trapped and emulated for the target environment. This causes a lot of performance overhead, as lots of instructions have to be trapped into the host/hypervisor and emulated.

Paravirtualization in the Case of XEN with Hypercalls

To avoid the performance problems related to binary translation when using full virtualization, we use paravirtualization, wherein the guest knows that it is running in a virtualized environment and its interaction with the host is optimized to avoid excessive trapping. As an example, the device driver code is changed and split into two parts. One is the back end, which is with the hypervisor, and the other is the front end, which is with the guest. The guest and host drivers now communicate over ring buffers.

The ring buffer is allocated from the guest memory. Now the guest can accumulate/aggregate data within the ring buffer and make one *hypercall* (i.e., a call to the hypervisor, also called a *kick*) to signal that the data is ready to be drained. This avoids excessive traps from the guest to the host and is a performance win.

In 2005, x86 finally became virtualizable. Intel introduced one more ring, called Ring -1, which is also called *virtual machine extensions (VMX) root mode*. The VMM runs in VMX root mode and the guests run in non-root mode.

This means that guests can run in Ring 0 and, for the majority of the instructions, there is no trap. Privileged/sensitive instructions that guests need are executed by the VMM in root mode via the trap. These switches are called *VM Exits* (i.e., the VMM takes over instruction executions from the guest) and *VM Entries* (the VM gains control from the VMM).

Apart from this, the virtualizable CPU manages a data structure called the VM control structure (VMCS), and it has the state of the VM and registers. The CPU uses this information during the VM Entries and Exits. The VMCS structure is like `task_struct`, the data structure used to represent a process. One VMCS pointer points to the currently active VMCS. When there is a trap to the VMM, VMCS provides the state of all the guest registers, like the reason of exit, and so on.

Advantages of hardware-assisted virtualization are two-fold:

- No binary translation

- No OS modification

The problem is that the VM Entries and Exits are still heavy calls involving a lot of CPU cycles, as the complete VM state has to be saved and restored. Considerable work has gone into reducing the cycles of these entries and exits. Using paravirtualized drivers helps mitigate some of these performance concerns. The details are explained in the next section.

IO Virtualization

There are generally two modes of IO virtualization:

- Full virtualization
- Paravirtualization

Full Virtualization

With full virtualization, the guest OS does not know that it's running on a hypervisor and doesn't need any changes to run on that hypervisor. Whenever the guest makes I/O calls, they are trapped on the hypervisor and the hypervisor performs the I/O on the physical device.

Paravirtualization

In this case, the guest OS is made aware that it's running in a virtualized environment and special drivers are loaded into the guest to take care of the I/O. The system calls for I/O are replaced with hypercalls.

Figure 1-1 shows the difference between paravirtualization and full virtualization.

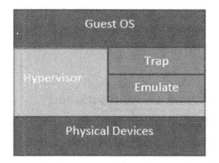 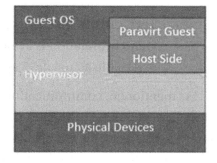

Figure 1-1. *Difference between full and paravirtualized drivers*

With the paravirtualized scenario, the guest-side drivers are called the front-end drivers and the host-side drivers are called the back-end drivers. Virtio is the virtualization standard for implementing paravirtualized drivers. The front-end network or I/O drivers of the guest are implemented based on the Virtio standard, and the front-end drivers are aware that they are running in a virtual environment. They work in tandem with the back-end Virtio drivers of the hypervisor. This working mechanism of front-end and back-end drivers helps achieve high-performance network and disk operations and is the reason for most of the performance benefits enjoyed by paravirtualization.

As mentioned, the front-end drivers on the guests implement a common set of interfaces, as described by the Virtio standard. When an I/O call has to be made from the process in the guest, the process invokes the front-end driver API and the driver passes the data packets to the corresponding back-end driver through the *virtqueue* (the virtual queue).

The back-end drivers can work in two ways:

- They can use QEMU emulation, which means the Quick Emulator (QEMU) emulates the device call via system calls from the user space. This means that the hypervisor lets the user-space QEMU program make the actual device calls.

- They can use mechanisms like *vhost*, whereby the QEMU emulation is avoided and the hypervisor kernel makes the actual device call.

As mentioned, communication between front-end and back-end Virtio drivers is done by the virtqueue abstraction. The virtqueue presents an API to interact with, which allows it to enqueue and dequeue buffers. Depending on the driver type, the driver can use zero or more queues. In the case of a network driver, it uses two virtqueues—one queue for the request and the other to receive the packets. The Virtio block driver, on the other hand, uses only one virtqueue.

Consider this example of a network packet flow, where the guest wants to send some data over the network:

1. The guest initiates a network packet write via the guest kernel.

2. The paravirtualized drivers (Virtio) in the guest take those buffers and put them into the virtqueue (tx).

3. The back end of the virtqueue is the worker thread, and it receives the buffers.

4. The buffers are then written to the tap device file descriptor. The tap device can be connected to a software bridge like an OVS or Linux bridge.

5. The other side of the bridge has a physical interface, which then takes the data out over the physical layer.

In this example, when a guest places the packets on the tx queue, it needs a mechanism to inform the host side that there are packets for handling. There is an interesting mechanism in Linux called eventfd that's used to notify the host side that there are events. The host watches the eventfd for changes.

A similar mechanism is used to send packets back to the guest.

As you saw in earlier sections, the hardware industry is catching up in the virtualization space and is providing more and more hardware virtualization, be it for CPUs (introducing a new ring) and instructions with vt-x or be it for memory (extended page tables).

Similarly, for I/O virtualization, hardware has a mechanism called an *I/O memory management unit*, which is similar to the CPU memory management unit (previously introduced) but is just for I/O-based memory. With the CPU MMU concept, the device memory access is intercepted and mapped to allow different guests. Guests are physically mapped to different physical memory and access is controlled by the I/O MMU hardware. This provides the isolation needed for device access.

This feature can be used in conjunction with something called *single root I/O virtualization (SRIOV)*, which allows an SRIOV-compatible device to be broken into multiple virtual functions. The basic idea is to bypass the hypervisor in the data path and use a pass-through mechanism, wherein the VM directly communicates with the devices. Details of SRIOV are beyond the scope of this book. Curious readers can follow these links for more about SRIOV:

https://blog.scottlowe.org/2009/12/02/what-is-sr-iov/

https://fir3net.com/Networking/Protocols/what-is-sr-iov-single-root-i-o-virtualization.html

Summary

In this chapter, we first delved into the history and evolution of virtualization. We explored its beginnings with IBM mainframes in the 1960s, followed by the introduction of UNIX and Java, which paved the way for process-level virtualization. The late 1990s saw VMware's entry into the virtualization scene, enabling the virtualization of actual hardware.

We next discussed two major virtualization techniques: VM-based virtualization, which virtualizes the entire OS, and container-based virtualization, which creates logical boundaries within the Linux kernel.

This chapter also explained the role of hypervisors, comprising the virtual machine monitor (VMM) and the device model, in managing the virtualized environments. We also examined memory and CPU virtualization techniques, such as shadow page tables and nested page tables with hardware support. Additionally, we explored the advantages of paravirtualization and Virtio drivers in optimizing I/O operations.

Overall, this chapter provided a comprehensive understanding of virtualization's key concepts and its importance in modern computing environments.

CHAPTER 2

Hypervisors

In Chapter 1, we discussed what virtualization is and covered the two types of virtualization—VM based and container based. The coverage of VM-based virtualization briefly discussed the role and importance of the hypervisor, which facilitates the creation of virtual machines.

In this chapter, we do a deep dive into hypervisors. Most of the chapter explains virtualization using components like the Linux Kernel Virtual Machine (KVM) and the Quick Emulator (QEMU). Based on these components, we then look at how VMs are created and how data flow between the guest and the hosts is facilitated.

Linux provides hypervisor facilities by using the QEMU in the user space and a specialized kernel module called the KVM (the Linux Kernel Virtual Machine). The KVM uses the Intel vt-x extension instruction set to isolate resources at the hardware level. Since the QEMU is a user-space process, the kernel treats it like other processes from a scheduling perspective.

Before we discuss the QEMU and KVM, let's touch upon Intel's vt-x and its specific instruction set.

The Intel Vt-x Instruction Set

Intel's virtualization technology (VT) comes in two flavors:

- Vt-x (for Intel x86 IA-32 and 64-bit architectures)

- Vt-i (for the Itanium processor line)

© Shashank Mohan Jain 2023
S. M. Jain, *Linux Containers and Virtualization*,
https://doi.org/10.1007/978-1-4842-9768-1_2

They are similar as far as functionalities. To understand the need for virtualization support at the CPU level, let's quickly review how programs and the OS interact with the CPU, as well as how programs in the VM interact with the CPU.

In the case of regular programs running on the host, the OS translates the program instructions into CPU instructions that are executed by the CPU.

In the case of a virtual machine, to run the programs within the VM, the guest OS translates program instructions into virtual CPU instructions and the hypervisor then converts these into instructions for the physical CPU.

As you can see, for the VM, the program instructions are translated twice—the program instructions are translated into virtual CPU instructions and the virtual CPU instructions are translated into physical CPU instructions.

This results in large performance overhead and slows down the VM. CPU virtualization, like the vt-x feature, enables complete abstraction of the full prowess of the CPU to the VM so that all the software in the VM can run without a performance hit; it runs as if it were on a dedicated CPU.

The vt-x also solves the problem whereby the x86 instructions architecture cannot be virtualized. According to the Popek and Goldberg principle for virtualization (https://en.wikipedia.org/wiki/Popek_and_Goldberg_virtualization_requirements), introduced in Chapter 1, all sensitive instructions must also be privileged. Privileged instructions cause a trap in user mode. In x86, some instructions are sensitive but not privileged. This means running them in the user space would not cause a trap. In effect, this means they are not virtualizable. An example of such an instruction is POPF.

vt-x simplifies the virtual machine monitor (VMM) software by closing virtualization holes by design:

- **Ring compression**: Without vt-x, the guest OS runs in Ring 1 and the guest OS apps run in Ring 3. To execute the privileged instructions in the guest OS, we need higher privileges, which are by default not available to the guest (due to security reasons). Therefore, to execute those instructions, we need to trap into the hypervisor (which runs in Ring 0 with more privileges), which can then execute the privileged instruction on behalf of the guest. This is called ring compression or deprivileging. vt-x avoids this by running the guest OS directly in Ring 0.

- **Non-trapping instructions**: Instructions like POPF on x86, which ideally should trap into the hypervisor because they are sensitive instructions, actually don't trap. This is a problem, as we need program control to shift to the hypervisor for all sensitive instructions. vt-x addresses this by running the guest OS in Ring 0, where instructions like POPF can trap into the hypervisor running in Ring -1.

- **Excessive trapping**: Without vt-x, all sensitive and privileged instructions trap into the hypervisor in Ring 0. With vt-x this becomes configurable and depends on the VMM as to which instructions cause a trap and which can be safely handled in Ring 0. Details of this are beyond the scope of this book.

vt-x adds two more modes: the non-root mode (in Ring -1) is where the VMM runs, and the root mode (in Ring 0) is where the guest OS runs.

To understand how these modes are involved in program execution, let's look at an example. Say that a program is being executed in a VM and, during the course of its execution, it makes a system call for I/O. As discussed in Chapter 1, guest programs in user space are executed in Ring 3. When the program makes an I/O call (which is a system call), these instructions are executed at the guest OS kernel level (Ring 0). The guest OS by itself cannot handle I/O calls, so it delegates them to the VMM (Ring -1). When the execution goes from Ring 0 to Ring -1, it's called a *VMExit*, and when the execution comes back from Ring -1 to Ring 0, it's called a *VMEntry*. This is all shown in Figure 2-1.

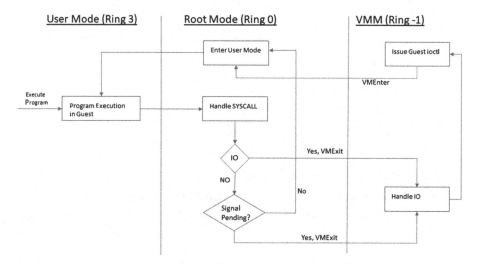

Figure 2-1. *Program execution in the guest with an I/O call*

Note   Before we dive into the QEMU, as a side note, I want to bring your attention to some interesting projects in virtualization, like Dune, which runs a process within the VM environment rather than a complete OS. In root mode, it's the VMM that runs. This is the mode where the KVM runs.

The Quick Emulator

The QEMU runs as a user process and handles the KVM kernel module. It uses the vt-x extensions to provide the guest with an isolated environment from a memory and CPU perspective. The QEMU process owns the guest RAM and is either memory mapped via a file or anonymous. Virtual CPUs are scheduled on the physical CPUs.

The main difference between a normal process and a QEMU process is the code executed on those threads. In the case of the guest, since it's the virtualized machine, the code executes the software BIOS and the operating system.

Figure 2-2 shows how the QEMU interacts with the hypervisor.

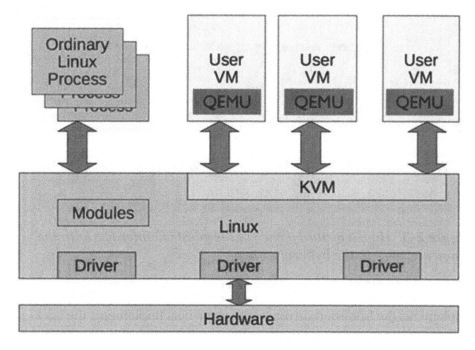

Figure 2-2. *QEMU interaction with the hypervisor*

The QEMU also dedicates a separate thread for I/O. This thread runs an event loop and is based on the non-blocking mechanism. It registers the file descriptors for I/O. The QEMU can use paravirtualized drivers like virtio to provide guests with virtio devices, such as `virtio-blk` for block devices and `virtio-net` for network devices. Figure 2-3 shows the specific components that facilitate communication between the guest and the host (hypervisor).

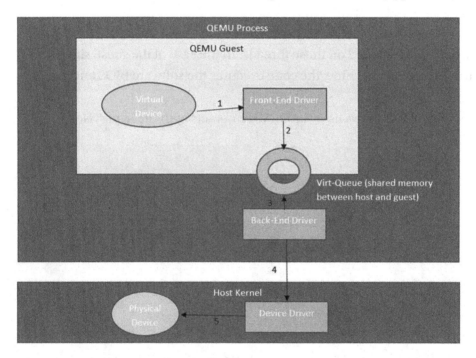

Figure 2-3. *How a virtual device in the guest OS interacts with the physical device in the hypervisor layer*

In Figure 2-3, you see that the guest within the QEMU process implements the front-end driver, whereas the host implements the back-end drivers. The communication between front-end and back-end drivers happens over specialized data structures, called *virtqueues*. Any packet that originates from the guest is first put into the virtqueue, and then the host-side driver is notified over a hypercall to drain the packet for actual processing to the device. There can be two variations of this packet flow, as follows:

- The packet from the guest is received by the QEMU and then pushed to the back-end driver on the host. One example is `virtio-net`.

- The packet from the guest directly reaches the host via what is called a *vhost driver*. This bypasses the QEMU layer and is relatively faster.

Creating a VM Using the KVM Module

To create a VM, a set of `ioctl` calls has to be made to the kernel KVM module, which exposes a `/dev/kvm` device to the guest. In simplistic terms, these are the calls from the user space to create and launch a VM:

1. `KVM CREATE VM`: This command creates a new VM that has no virtual CPUs and no memory.

2. `KVM SET USER MEMORY REGION`: This command maps the user-space memory for the VM.

3. `KVM CREATE IRQCHIP` / `KVM CREATE VCPU`: This command creates a hardware component like a virtual CPU and maps them with `vt-x` functionalities.

4. `KVM SET REGS` / `SREGS` / `KVM SET FPU` / `KVM SET CPUID` / `KVM SET MSRS` / `KVM SET VCPU EVENTS` / `KVM SET LAPIC`: These commands are hardware configurations.

5. `KVM RUN`: This command starts the VM.

KVM RUN starts the VM and internally is the VMLaunch instruction invoked by the KVM kernel module that puts the VM code execution into non-root mode. It then changes the instruction pointer to the code location in the guest's memory. This is a slight oversimplification, as the module does much more to set up the VM, including setting up the VMCS (VM Control Structure), and so on.

Vhost-Based Data Communication

Any discussion about hypervisors would be incomplete without showing a concrete example. We'll look at an example of a network packet flow (depicted in Figure 2-4) in the context of the vhost-net device drivers. When we use the vhost mechanism, the QEMU is out of the data plane and there is direct communication between the guest and host over virtqueues. The QEMU remains in the control plane, where it sets up the vhost device on the kernel using the ioctl command:

```
/dev/vhost-net device
```

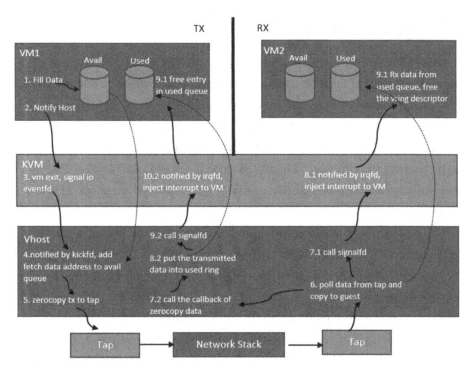

Figure 2-4. *Network packet flow*

When the device is initialized, a kernel thread is created for the specific QEMU process. This thread handles the I/O for the specific guest. The thread listens to events on the host side, on the virtqueues. When an event arrives to drain the data (in virtio terminology, it's called a *kick (hypercall)*), the I/O thread drains the packet from the tx (transmission) queue of the guest. The thread then transmits this data to the tap device, which it makes it available to the underlying bridge/switch in order to transmit it downstream to an overlay or routing mechanism.

The KVM kernel module registers the eventfd for the guest. This a file descriptor that's registered for the guest (by the QEMU) with the KVM kernel module. The FD is registered against a guest I/O exit event (a kick), which drains the data.

What Is an eventfd?

An *eventfd* is an interprocess communication (IPC) mechanism that offers a wait-notify facility between user-space programs or between the kernel and the user space. The idea is simple. In the same way that we have file descriptors for files, we can create file descriptors for events. The benefit here is that the FDs can then be treated like other FDs and can be registered with mechanisms like `poll`, `select`, and `epoll`. The mechanisms can then facilitate a notification system when those FDs are written to.

The consumer thread can be made to wait on an epoll object via `epoll_wait`. Once the producer thread writes to the FD, the epoll mechanism will notify the consumer (again depending on the edge or level triggers) of the event.

Edge-triggered means that you only get notified when the event is detected (which takes place, say instantaneously), while *level-triggered* means you get notified when the event is present (which will be true over a period of time).

For example, in an edge-triggered system, if you want a notification to signal you when data is available to read, you'll only get that notification when data was not available to read before but now is. If you read some of the available data (so that some of the data is still available to read), you will not get another notification. If you read all of the available data, you will get another notification when new data becomes available to read again. In a level-triggered system, you'd get that notification whenever data is available to read.

The host uses an `eventfd` by using `ioeventfd` to send data from the guest to the host and `irqfd` to receive an interrupt from the host to the guest.

Another use case for eventfds is the out of memory (OOM) cgroup. The way this works is that whenever the process exceeds the memcg limit, the OOM killer can decide to kill it or, if this behavior is disabled, the kernel can do the following

1. Create the eventfd.

2. Write the OOM event to the eventfd.

The process thread will block until the event is generated. Once the event is generated, the thread is woken up to react to the OOM notification.

The difference between eventfd and a Linux pipe is that the pipe needs two file descriptors, whereas eventfd just needs one.

The vhost I/O thread watches for the eventfd. Whenever the I/O event happens from the guest, the I/O thread for the guest gets informed that it has to drain the buffers from the tx queue.

Similar to ioeventfd, there is an irqfd. The QEMU user space also registers this (irqfd) FD for the guest. The guest driver listens for changes to those FDs. The reason for using this is to pass interrupts back to the guest to notify the guest-side driver to process the packets. Taking the previous example, when the packets have to be sent back to the guest, the I/O thread fills up the rx queue (the receive queue) buffers for the guest and the interrupt injection is done to the guest via irqfd. In the reverse path of packet flow, the packets received on the host over the physical interface are sent to the tap device. The thread that's interfacing with the tap device receives the packets to fill up the rx buffers for the guest. It then notifies the guest driver over irqfds. Figure 2-4 shows this process.

Alternative Virtualization Mechanisms

Having covered virtualization via VM-based mechanisms, it's time to briefly look at other means of virtualization that depart from container isolation, like the namespaces/cgroups-based mechanism that Docker uses. The point of this section is to understand that it is possible to do the following:

- Reduce the interfaces exposed by different software layers like the VMM in order to reduce attack vectors. The attack vectors can come in the form of exploits, like memory exploits that install malicious software or control the system by elevating privileges.

- Use hardware isolation to isolate the different containers/processes we run.

In summary, we can get the isolation levels of VMs with a reduced or minimalistic exposed machine interface and with a provisioning speed similar to that of containers.

We have already discussed how VMs, with the help of the VMM, isolate these workloads. The VMM exposes the machine model (x86 interface), whereas the container exposes the POSIX interface. The VMM, with hardware virtualization, can isolate CPU, memory, and I/O (vt-d, SRIOV, and IOMMU). Containers that share the kernel provide this feature via namespaces and cgroups, but are still considered a weaker alternative to the hardware-based isolation techniques.

So, is there a way to get the two worlds closer? One of the goals would be to reduce the attack vector by employing a minimalistic interface approach. What this means is that, instead of exposing complete POSIX API to apps or a complete machine interface to the guest OS, we provide only what the app/OS needs. This is where we started to see the evolution of how the unikernel and the library OS started to happen.

Unikernels

Unikernels provide the mechanism, via toolchains, for preparing a minimalistic OS. This means that if the application only needs network

APIs, then the keyboard, mouse devices, and their drivers are not packaged. This reduces the attack vector considerably.

One of the early problems with unikernels was that they had to be built across different models of device drivers. With the advent of I/O virtualization and virtio drivers, this problem is somewhat resolved, as the unikernels can now be built with exact virtio devices and the drivers needed for the apps on the guest. This means the guest can be a unikernel (library OS) sitting on top of, say, a hypervisor like KVM. This still has limitations, as the QEMU or the user-space part still has a good amount of codebase, all of which is subject to exploits.

To achieve further minimalism, one solution is to package the VMM alongside the unikernel, meaning the VMM now plays the role of the QEMU for the unikernel, but per instance. The VMM code is limited to the needed functionality and facilitates memory-based communication between the guest and the VMM. With this model, multiple VMMs can be made to sit on the hypervisor. The VMM role facilitates I/O and creates the guest unikernel using the hardware isolation capabilities.

The unikernel itself is a single process with no multithreading capabilities, as shown in Figure 2-5.

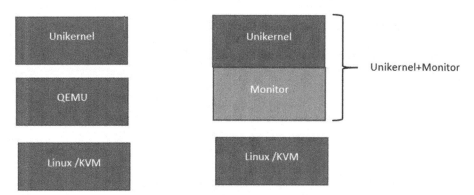

Figure 2-5. *The unikernel is a single process with no multithreading capabilities*

In Figure 2-5, observe that the image on the left is running a VMM and the QEMU combined, to run unikernels on top, whereas the image on the right shows a VMM (monitor) like UKVM packaged alongside the unikernel. So basically we have reduced the code (the QEMU) and thereby have eliminated a significant attack vector. This is in line with the minimalistic interfaces approach we talked about previously.

Project Dune

A careful reader can easily make out that the vt-x isolation on the memory and CPU is not opinionated about running only a guest OS code in the guest's memory. Technically, we can provision different sandboxing mechanisms on top of this hardware isolation. This is precisely what Project Dune does. On top of the hardware isolation of vt-x, Dune doesn't spin a guest OS, but rather a Linux process. This means the process is made to run in Ring 0 of the CPU and has the machine interface exposed to it. The process can be made to sandbox by

1. Running the trusted code of the process in Ring 0.
    This is basically the library that Dune calls libdune.

2. Running the untrusted code in Ring 3.

The Dune architecture is shown in Figure 2-6.

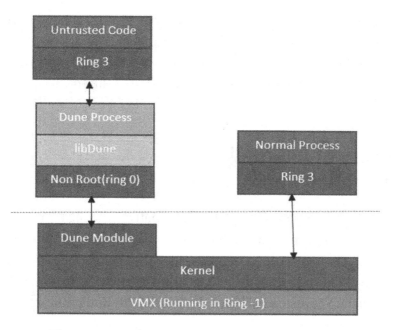

Figure 2-6. *The Dune architecture*

To bootstrap the process, Dune creates an operating environment, which entails setting up the page tables (the CR3 register is pointing to the root). It also sets up the interrupt descriptor table (IDT) for the hardware exceptions. The trusted and untrusted code runs in the same address space, wherein the memory pages of the trusted code are protected by supervisor bits in page table entries. The system calls trap into the same process and are interposed with hypercalls to the VMM. For more details on Dune, check out `http://dune.scs.stanford.edu/`.

novm

novm is another type of hardware container and also is an alternate form of virtualization. (It also uses the KVM APIs to create the VM by using the /dev/kvm device file.) Instead of presenting a disk interface to the VM, novm presents a file system (9p) interface to the VM. This allows packaging of software that we want to provision as a container. There is no BIOS, and the VMM simply puts the VM in 32-bit protected mode directly. This makes the provisioning process faster, because steps like device probing are not needed.

Summary of Alternative Virtualization Approaches

In summary, this section covered three alternative virtualization approaches: the first approach packages a unikernel with a minimal OS interface, the second approach gets rid of the OS interface and runs a process within Ring 0 directly, and the third approach provides a file system into the VM instead of block devices directly and optimizes booting aspects.

These approaches provide good isolation at the hardware level and very fast spin-up times, and they might be a good fit for running serverless workloads and other cloud workloads.

Do other approaches exit? Of course. Companies like Cloudflare and Fastly are trying to address virtualization by offering isolation within a process. The intent is to use the capabilities of certain languages to have the following:

- Code flow isolation via control flow integrity

- Memory isolation

- Capability-based security

We could then use these primitives to build sandboxes within each process itself. This way, we can get even faster boot times for the code we want to execute.

WebAssembly is leading the innovation in this space. The basic idea is to run WebAssembly, a.k.a. Wasm modules, within the same process (the WASM runtime). Each module is isolated from the other modules, so we get one sandbox per tenant. This fits well into the serverless computer paradigms and probably prevents problems like cold start.

On a side note, there is a new functionality called *hotplug capability* that makes the devices dynamically available in the guest. The hot plugging capability allows developers to dynamically resize the block devices, as an example, without restarting the guest. There is also the `hotplug-dimm` module, which allows developers to resize the RAM available to the guest.

Summary

This chapter focused on Linux's hypervisor facilities, particularly the QEMU and the KVM. The KVM utilizes Intel's vt-x extension instruction set to achieve hardware-level resource isolation. By running the QEMU in user space, the kernel treats it as any other process from a scheduling perspective. The Intel vt-x instruction set consists of two flavors: Vt-x for Intel x86 IA-32 and 64-bit architectures, and Vt-i for the Itanium processor line. The need for CPU virtualization support arises from the fact that VMs require translating program instructions twice, resulting in performance overhead. Vt-x simplifies the VMM software by running the guest OS directly in Ring 0, avoiding ring compression and excessive trapping.

The QEMU operates as a user process and interfaces with the KVM kernel module, utilizing vt-x extensions to isolate the guest's environment in terms of memory and CPU. The QEMU owns the guest RAM, which can be either memory-mapped via a file or anonymous. The QEMU also handles I/O through a separate thread using paravirtualized drivers like virtio to provide virtual devices to guests. Communication between the guest OS and the host occurs over specialized data structures called virtqueues.

Creating a VM using the KVM module involves a set of `ioctl` calls from user space to create and launch a VM. `KVM RUN` starts the VM, putting it into non-root mode using the VMLaunch instruction, which sets the guest's code execution in motion.

The chapter also briefly touched upon alternative virtualization mechanisms, such as unikernels, which package minimalistic OS interfaces, and Project Dune, which runs a Linux process in Ring 0 without spinning up a guest OS. Furthermore, novm provides hardware containers with a file system interface, optimizing booting processes. These approaches offer good hardware-level isolation and fast spin-up times, making them suitable for cloud workloads and serverless environments. The chapter concluded by mentioning innovative approaches like Cloudflare and Fastly, using control flow integrity, memory isolation, and capability-based security to build sandboxes within processes themselves, potentially achieving even faster boot times for executed code, especially with the rise of WebAssembly (Wasm) modules.

CHAPTER 3

Namespaces

In this chapter, we touch upon an important aspect of Linux containers, called Linux namespaces. Namespaces allow the kernel to provide isolation by restricting the visibility of the kernel resources like mount points, network subsystems among processes scoped to different namespaces.

Today, containers are the de facto cloud software provisioning mechanism. Containers provide fast spin-up times and have less overhead than virtual machines. There are certain very specific reasons behind these features.

As introduced in Chapter 1, VM-based virtualization emulates the hardware and provides an OS as the abstraction. This means that a bulk of the OS code and the device drivers are loaded as part of the provisioning. By contrast, containers virtualize the OS itself. This means that there are data structures within the kernel that facilitate this separation. Most of the time, we are not clear as to what is happening behind the covers.

Linux containers are made of three Linux kernel primitives:

- Linux namespaces

- Cgroups (covered in depth in Chapter 4)

- Layered file systems (covered in depth in Chapter 5)

© Shashank Mohan Jain 2023
S. M. Jain, *Linux Containers and Virtualization*,
https://doi.org/10.1007/978-1-4842-9768-1_3

A *namespace* is a data structure which provides logical isolation within the Linux kernel. A namespace controls visibility within the kernel. All the controls are defined at the process level. That means a namespace controls which resources within the kernel a process can see. Think of the Linux kernel as a guard protecting resources like OS memory, privileged CPU instructions, disks, and other resources that only the kernel should be able to access. Applications running within user space should only access these resources via a trap, in which case the kernel takes over control and executes these instructions on behalf of the user space–based applications. As an example, an application that wants to access a file on a disk has to delegate this call to the kernel via a system call (which internally traps into the kernel) to the Linux kernel, which then executes this request on behalf of the application.

Since there could be many user space–based applications running in parallel on a single Linux kernel, we need a way to provide isolation between these user space–based applications. *Isolation* means that there should be some kind of sandboxing of the individual application so that certain resources in the application are confined to that sandbox. As an example, we would like to have a file system sandbox, which would mean that within that sandbox, we could have our own view of the files. That way, multiple such sandboxes could be run over the same Linux kernel without interfering with each other.

Sandboxing is achieved by using *namespaces*.

Namespace Types

This section explains the different namespaces that exist within the Linux kernel and discusses how they are realized within the kernel.

UTS

This namespace allows a process to see a separate hostname other than the hostname within the global namespace of the host.

PID

The processes within the PID namespace have a different process tree. They have an init process with PID 1. At the data-structure level, though, the processes belong to one global process tree, which is visible only at the host level. Tools like ps or direct usage of the /proc file system from within the namespace will list the processes and their related resources for the process tree within the namespace.

Mount

Mount is one of the most important namespaces. It controls which mount points a process should be able to see. If a process is within a namespace, it can only see the mounts within that namespace.

A small detour might be of help to explain how mount propagation works with containers. A mount in the kernel is represented by a data structure called vfsmount. All mounts form a tree-like structure, with a child mount structure holding a reference to the parent mount structure.

All code displayed here is taken from Linux Kernel 4.15.18:

```
struct vfsmount {
      struct list_head mnt_hash;
      struct vfsmount *mnt_parent;    /* fs we are mounted on */
      struct dentry *mnt_mountpoint;  /* dentry of mountpoint */
      struct dentry *mnt_root;      /* root of the
      mounted tree*/
```

```
        struct super_block *mnt_sb;        /* pointer to
        superblock */
        struct list_head mnt_mounts;  /* list of children,
                                            anchored here */
        struct list_head mnt_child;       /* and going through
        their mnt_child */
        atomic_t mnt_count;
        int mnt_flags;
        char *mnt_devname;                    /* Name of device e.g.
                                                /dev/dsk/hda1 */
        struct list_head mnt_list;
};
```

Whenever a mount operation is invoked, a vfsmount structure is created and the *dentry* of the mount point as well as the *dentry* of the mounted tree are populated. A *dentry* is a data structure that maps the inode to the filename.

Apart from mount, there is a *bind mount,* which allows a directory (instead of a device) to be mounted at a mount point. The process of bind mounting results in creating a vfsmount structure that points to the *dentry* of the directory.

Containers work on the concept of bind mounts. So, when a volume is created for a container, it's actually a bind mount of a directory within the host to a mount point within the container's file system. Since the mount happens within the mount namespace, the vfsmount structures are scoped to the mount namespace. This means that, by creating a bind mount of a directory, we can expose a volume within the namespace that's holding the container.

Network

A network namespace gives a container a separate set of network subsystems. This means that the process within the network namespace will see different network interfaces, routes, and iptables. This separates the container network from the host network. We will study this in more depth in Chapter 6 when we look at an example of the packet flow between two containers in different namespaces on the same host as well as containers in different namespaces within the same host.

IPC

This namespace scopes IPC constructs such as POSIX message queues. Between two processes within the same namespace, IPC is enabled, but it will be restricted if two processes in two different namespaces try to communicate over IPC.

Cgroup

This namespace restricts the visibility of the cgroup file system to the cgroup the process belongs to. Without this restriction, a process could peek at the global cgroups via the /proc/self/cgroup hierarchy. This namespace effectively virtualizes the cgroup itself.

Apart from the namespaces mentioned here, as of the writing of this there is one more namespace called the time namespace.

Time

The time namespace has two main use cases:

- Changes the date and time inside a container

- Adjusts the clocks for a container restored from a checkpoint

The kernel provides access to several clocks: CLOCK_REALTIME, CLOCK_MONOTONIC, and CLOCK_BOOTTIME. The latter two clocks are monotonic, but the start points for them are not well defined (currently start point is system startup time, but the POSIX says "since an unspecified point in the past") and are different for each system. When a container migrates from one node to another, all the clocks are restored to their consistent states. In other words, they have to continue running from the same point at which they were dumped.

Data Structures for Linux Namespaces

Now that you have a basic idea about namespaces, you are prepared to study the details about how some of the data structures in the Linux kernel allow this separation when it comes to Linux containers. The term used for these structures is *Linux namespaces.*

The kernel represents each process as a task_struct data structure. The following shows details of this structure and lists some of its members:

```
/* task_struct member predeclarations (sorted
alphabetically): */
struct audit_context;
struct backing_dev_info;
struct bio_list;
struct blk_plug;
struct capture_control;
```

```
struct cfs_rq;
struct fs_struct;
struct futex_pi_state;
struct io_context;
struct mempolicy;
struct nameidata;
struct nsproxy;
struct perf_event_context;
struct pid_namespace;
struct pipe_inode_info;
struct rcu_node;
struct reclaim_state;
struct robust_list_head;
struct root_domain;
struct rq;
struct sched_attr;
struct sched_param;
struct seq_file;
struct sighand_struct;
struct signal_struct;
struct task_delay_info;
struct task_group;
```

The nsproxy structure is a holder structure for the different namespaces that a task (process) belongs to:

```
struct nsproxy {
        atomic_t count;
        struct uts_namespace *uts_ns;
        struct ipc_namespace *ipc_ns;
        struct mnt_namespace *mnt_ns;
        struct pid_namespace *pid_ns_for_children;
        struct net            *net_ns;
```

```
        struct time_namespace *time_ns;
        struct time_namespace *time_ns_for_children;
        struct cgroup_namespace *cgroup_ns;
};
extern struct nsproxy init_nsproxy;
```

The nsproxy structure holds the eight namespace data structures. The missing one is the user namespace, which is part of the cred data structure in the task_struct.

There are three system calls that can be used to put tasks into specific namespaces: clone, unshare, and setns. The clone and setns calls result in creating a nsproxy object and then adding the specific namespaces needed for the task.

For purposes of illustration, the remainder of this section focuses specifically on network namespaces. A network namespace is represented by a net structure. Part of that data structure is shown here:

```
struct net {
        /* First cache line can be often dirtied.
         * Do not place read-mostly fields here.
         */
        refcount_t              passive;        /* To decide when
                                                   the network
                                                 * namespace should
                                                   be freed.
                                                 */
        refcount_t              count;          /* To decide when
                                                   the network
                                                 *  namespace should
                                                   be shut down.
                                                 */
        spinlock_t              rules_mod_lock;
        unsigned int            dev_unreg_count;
```

```
    unsigned int          dev_base_seq;    /* protected by
                                            rtnl_mutex */

    int                   ifindex;
    spinlock_t            nsid_lock;
    atomic_t              fnhe_genid;
    struct list_head      list;            /* list of network
                                            namespaces */

    struct list_head      exit_list;       /* To linked to
                                            call pernet exit
                                            * methods on
                                            dead net (
                                            * pernet_ops_rwsem
                                            read locked),
                                            * or to unregister
                                            pernet ops
                                            * (pernet_ops_rwsem
                                            write locked).
                                            */
    struct llist_node     cleanup_list;    /* namespaces on
                                            death row */
#ifdef CONFIG_KEYS
    struct key_tag             *key_domain; /* Key domain of
                                            operation tag */
#endif
    struct user_namespace      *user_ns;    /* Owning user
                                            namespace */

    struct ucounts             *ucounts;
    struct idr                 netns_ids;
    struct ns_common      ns;
    struct list_head      dev_base_head;
    struct proc_dir_entry      *proc_net;
```

```
        struct proc_dir_entry      *proc_net_stat;
#ifdef CONFIG_SYSCTL
        struct ctl_table_set        sysctls;
#endif
        struct sock                 *rtnl;          /* rtnetlink
                                                       socket */

        struct sock                 *genl_sock;
        struct uevent_sock          *uevent_sock;   /* uevent
                                                          socket */
        struct hlist_head           *dev_name_head;
        struct hlist_head           *dev_index_head;
        struct raw_notifier_head     netdev_chain;
```

One of the elements of this data structure is the user namespace to which this network namespace belongs. Apart from that, the major structural part of this is net_ns_ipv4, which includes the routing table, net filter rules, and so on:

```
struct netns_ipv4 {
#ifdef CONFIG_SYSCTL
        struct ctl_table_header     *forw_hdr;
        struct ctl_table_header     *frags_hdr;
        struct ctl_table_header     *ipv4_hdr;
        struct ctl_table_header     *route_hdr;
        struct ctl_table_header     *xfrm4_hdr;
#endif
        struct ipv4_devconf         *devconf_all;
        struct ipv4_devconf         *devconf_dflt;
        struct ip_ra_chain __rcu *ra_chain;
        struct mutex             ra_mutex;
#ifdef CONFIG_IP_MULTIPLE_TABLES
        struct fib_rules_ops *rules_ops;
```

```
    bool                        fib_has_custom_rules;
    unsigned int                fib_rules_require_fldissect;
    struct fib_table __rcu     *fib_main;
    struct fib_table __rcu     *fib_default;
#endif
    bool                        fib_has_custom_local_routes;
#ifdef CONFIG_IP_ROUTE_CLASSID
    Int                         fib_num_tclassid_users;
#endif
    struct hlist_head      *fib_table_hash;
    bool                        fib_offload_disabled;
    struct sock            *fibnl;
    struct sock  * __percpu    *icmp_sk;
    struct sock            *mc_autojoin_sk;
    struct inet_peer_base     *peers;
    struct sock  * __percpu    *tcp_sk;
    struct fqdir          *fqdir;
#ifdef CONFIG_NETFILTER
    struct xt_table       *iptable_filter;
    struct xt_table       *iptable_mangle;
    struct xt_table       *iptable_raw;
    struct xt_table       *arptable_filter;
#ifdef CONFIG_SECURITY
    struct xt_table       *iptable_security;
#endif
    struct xt_table       *nat_table;
#endif
    int sysctl_icmp_echo_ignore_all;
    int sysctl_icmp_echo_ignore_broadcasts;
    int sysctl_icmp_ignore_bogus_error_responses;
    int sysctl_icmp_ratelimit;
```

```
int sysctl_icmp_ratemask;
int sysctl_icmp_errors_use_inbound_ifaddr;
struct local_ports ip_local_ports;
int sysctl_tcp_ecn;
int sysctl_tcp_ecn_fallback;
int sysctl_ip_default_ttl;
int sysctl_ip_no_pmtu_disc;
int sysctl_ip_fwd_use_pmtu;
int sysctl_ip_fwd_update_priority;
int sysctl_ip_nonlocal_bind;
int sysctl_ip_autobind_reuse;
/* Shall we try to damage output packets if routing dev
changes? */
int sysctl_ip_dynaddr;
```

This is how the iptables and routing rules are all scoped into the network namespace.

Other data structures of relevance here are the net_device (this is how the kernel represents the network card/device) and sock (a kernel representation of a socket data structure). These two structures allow the device to be scoped into a network namespace as well as the socket to be scoped to the namespace. Both these structures can be part of only one namespace at a time. We can move the device to a different namespace via the iproute2 utility.

Here are some of the user-space commands to handle the network namespaces:

- Ip netns add testns: Adds a network namespace

- Ip netns del testns: Deletes the mentioned namespace

- Ip netns exec testns sh: Executes a shell within the testns namespace

Adding a Device to a Namespace

To add a device to a namespace, first create a veth pair device (this device can be used to join two namespaces):

```
ip link add veth0 type veth peer name veth1
```

Then add one end of the veth pair to the network namespace testns:

```
ip link set veth1 netns testns
```

The other end (veth0) is in the host namespace, so any traffic sent to veth0 ends up on veth1 in the testns namespace.

Assume that we run an HTTP server in the testns namespace, which means the listener socket is scoped to the testns namespace, as explained previously in the sock data structure. So, a TCP packet to be delivered to the IP and port of the application within the testns namespace would be delivered to the socket scoped within that namespace.

This is how the kernel virtualizes the operating system and various subsystems like networking, IPC, mounts, and so on.

Summary

In this chapter, you learned about the Linux namespaces and how they facilitate isolation between user space–based applications. We also looked into how different Linux kernel-based data structures are used to realize the different namespaces. Going forward, we will look into how the Linux kernel provides resource limits to the different user space–based processes so that one process doesn't hog the resources of the operating system.

CHAPTER 4

Cgroups

In Chapter 3, you learned how to control visibility of Linux processes by using namespaces and learned how they are realized within the kernel. In this chapter, we explore another important aspect—resource control—which enables us to apply quotas to various kernel resources.

As you learned in Chapter 3, namespaces enable us to restrict the visibility of resources for processes, which we did by putting the processes in separate namespaces. Chapter 3 also covered the data structures involved in the kernel, to give you an understanding of how a namespace is realized within the Linux kernel.

Now we address the question, "Is restricting visibility good enough for virtualization, or do we need to do more"? Assume we run `tenant1` processes in one namespace and `tenant2` processes in a separate namespace. Although the processes can't access each other's resources (mount points, process trees, and so on), as those resources are scoped to the individual namespace, we don't achieve true isolation just via this scoping.

As an example, what stops `tenant1` from launching a process that possibly could hog the CPU via an infinite loop? Flawed code can keep leaking memory (say, for example, it takes a big chunk of the OS page cache). A misbehaving process can create tons of processes via forking, launch a fork bomb, and crash the kernel.

© Shashank Mohan Jain 2023
S. M. Jain, *Linux Containers and Virtualization*,
https://doi.org/10.1007/978-1-4842-9768-1_4

This means we need a way to introduce resource controls for processes within the namespace. This is achieved using a mechanism called *control groups,* commonly known as *cgroups.* Cgroups work on the concept of cgroup controllers and are represented by a file system called `cgroupfs` in the Linux kernel.

The version of cgroups currently being used is cgroup v2. In this chapter we explore some details about how cgroups work as well as some of the cgroup controllers that exist in the kernel code. We also look at how the cgroups are realized within the Linux kernel. But before that, let's briefly see what cgroups are all about.

First, to use the cgroup, we need to mount the `cgroup` file system at a mount point, as follows:

```
mount -t cgroup2 none $MOUNT_POINT
```

The difference between cgroup version v1 and v2 is that, while mounting in v1, we could have specified the mount options to specify the controllers to enable, in cgroup v2, no such mount option can be passed.

Creating a Sample Cgroup

Let's create a sample cgroup called `mygrp`. To create a cgroup, we first need to create a folder where the cgroup artifacts are stored, as follows:

```
mkdir mygrp
```

Now we can create a cgroup using the following commands:

Note   cgroup2 is supported in kernel version 4.12.0-rc5 onward. I am working on Ubuntu 20.04.6 LTS, which has kernel version 5.15.0.

```
mount -t cgroup2 none mygrp
```

```
root@osboxes:~# mkdir mygrp
root@osboxes:~# mount -t cgroup2 none mygrp
root@osboxes:~# cd mygrp
root@osboxes:~/mygrp# ls -l
total 0
-r--r--r--  1 root root 0 Jul  2 00:29 cgroup.controllers
-rw-r--r--  1 root root 0 Jul  2 00:29 cgroup.max.depth
-rw-r--r--  1 root root 0 Jul  2 00:29 cgroup.max.descendants
-rw-r--r--  1 root root 0 Jul  2 00:29 cgroup.procs
-r--r--r--  1 root root 0 Jul  2 00:29 cgroup.stat
-rw-r--r--  1 root root 0 Jul  2 00:29 cgroup.subtree_control
-rw-r--r--  1 root root 0 Jul  2 00:29 cgroup.threads
drwxr-xr-x  2 root root 0 Jul  2 00:29 init.scope
drwxr-xr-x 52 root root 0 Jul  2 00:29 system.slice
drwxr-xr-x  4 root root 0 Jul  2 00:25 user.slice
root@osboxes:~/mygrp# 
```

We created a directory called mygrp and then mounted the cgroup v2 file system on it. When we navigate inside the mygrp directory, we can see multiple files there:

- cgroup.controllers: This file contains the supported controllers. All controllers that are not mounted on cgroup v1 will show up. Currently on my system, I have a cgroup v1 mounted by systemd. The following shows that all the controllers are there:

```
root@osboxes:~/mygrp# mount | grep cgroup
tmpfs on /sys/fs/cgroup type tmpfs (ro,nosuid,nodev,noexec,mode=755)
cgroup2 on /sys/fs/cgroup/unified type cgroup2 (rw,nosuid,nodev,noexec,relatime)
cgroup on /sys/fs/cgroup/systemd type cgroup (rw,nosuid,nodev,noexec,relatime,xattr,name=systemd)
cgroup on /sys/fs/cgroup/blkio type cgroup (rw,nosuid,nodev,noexec,relatime,blkio)
cgroup on /sys/fs/cgroup/memory type cgroup (rw,nosuid,nodev,noexec,relatime,memory)
cgroup on /sys/fs/cgroup/perf_event type cgroup (rw,nosuid,nodev,noexec,relatime,perf_event)
cgroup on /sys/fs/cgroup/cpu,cpuacct type cgroup (rw,nosuid,nodev,noexec,relatime,cpu,cpuacct)
cgroup on /sys/fs/cgroup/hugetlb type cgroup (rw,nosuid,nodev,noexec,relatime,hugetlb)
cgroup on /sys/fs/cgroup/devices type cgroup (rw,nosuid,nodev,noexec,relatime,devices)
cgroup on /sys/fs/cgroup/freezer type cgroup (rw,nosuid,nodev,noexec,relatime,freezer)
cgroup on /sys/fs/cgroup/cpuset type cgroup (rw,nosuid,nodev,noexec,relatime,cpuset)
none on /root/mygrp type cgroup2 (rw,relatime)
```

Only after unmounting the controllers from v1 should v2 show these controllers. Sometimes we might need to add the kernel boot parameter `systemd.unified_cgroup_hierarchy=1` and reboot the kernel to make these changes effective. After making the changes on my machine, I see the following controllers:

```
root@osboxes:~# mount -t cgroup2 none mygrp
root@osboxes:~# cd mygrp/
root@osboxes:~/mygrp# ls
cgroup.controllers  cgroup.max.depth  cgroup.max.descendants  cgro
root@osboxes:~/mygrp# cat cgroup.controllers
cpu io memory
root@osboxes:~/mygrp# |
```

- `cgroup.procs`: This file contains the processes within the root cgroup. No PIDs will be there when the cgroup is freshly created. By writing the PIDs to this file, they become part of the cgroup.

- `cgroup.subtree_control`: This holds controllers that are enabled for the immediate subgroup.

  Enabling and disabling controllers in the immediate subgroups of a parent is done only by writing into its `cgroup.subtree_control` file. So, for example, enabling the memory controller is done using this:

  `echo "+memory" > mygrp/cgroup.subtree_control`

  And disabling it is done using this:

  echo "-memory" > mygrp/cgroup.subtree_control

- `cgroup.events`: This is the cgroup core interface file. This interface file is unique to non-root subgroups. The `cgroup.events` file reflects the number of processes attached to the subgroup, and it consists of one item—populated: value. The value is 0 when there are no processes attached to that subgroup or its descendants, and 1 when there are one or more processes attached to that subgroup or its descendants.

Apart from these files, controller-specific interface files are also created. As an example, for memory controllers, a memory.events file is created, which can be monitored for events like out of memory (OOM). Similarly, a PID controller has files like pids.max to avoid situations like a fork bomb.

In my example, I created a child cgroup under mygrp. The following files appear under the child directory:

```
root@osboxes:~/mygrp# cd child/
root@osboxes:~/mygrp/child# ls
cgroup.controllers  cgroup.max.depth        cgroup.procs  cgroup.subtree_control
cgroup.events       cgroup.max.descendants  cgroup.stat   cgroup.threads
```

```
cgroup.subtree_control cgroup.type cpu.stat      cpu.weight.nice io.stat    memory.current memory.high memory.max memory.oom.group
cgroup.threads         cpu.max     cpu.weight    io.max          io.weight  memory.events  memory.low  memory.min memory.stat
```

We can see controller-specific files like memory.max. The interface file called memory.events lists the different events like oom, which can be enabled and disabled:

```
root@osboxes:~/mygrp/child# cat memory.events
low 0
high 0
max 0
oom 0
oom_kill 0
```

The next section explains how cgroups are implemented within the kernel and how they enable resource control.

Cgroup Types

There are different types of cgroups, based on which resources we want to control. The two types of cgroups we will cover here are as follows:

- **CPU**: Provides CPU limits to user-space processes

- **Block I/O**: Provides I/O limits on block devices for user-space processes

CPU Cgroup

From the kernel perspective, let's see how a cgroup is realized. CPU cgroups can be realized on top of two schedulers:

- Completely fair scheduler

- Real-time scheduler

In this chapter, we discuss only the completely fair scheduler (CFS). The CPU cgroup provides different types of CPU resource control:

- cpu.shares: Contains an integer value that specifies a relative share of CPU time available to the tasks in a cgroup. For example, tasks in two cgroups that have cpu.shares set to 100 will receive equal CPU time, but tasks in a cgroup that have cpu.shares set to 200 receive twice the CPU time of the tasks in a cgroup where cpu.shares is set to 100. The value specified in the cpu.shares file must be 2 or higher.

- cpu.cfs_quota_us: Specifies the total amount of time in microseconds (µs, represented here as "us") for which all tasks in a cgroup can run during one period (as defined by cpu.cfs_period_us). As soon as tasks in a cgroup use all the time specified by the quota, they are stopped for the remainder of the time specified by the period and not allowed to run until the next period.

- `cpu.cfs_period_us`: Specifies the period from which CPU quotas for cgroups (`cpu.cfs_quota_us`) are carved out and the quota and period parameters operate on a per CPU basis. Consider these examples:

  - To allow the cgroup to be able to access a single CPU for 0.2 second of every second, set `cpu.cfs_quota_us` to 200000 and `cpu.cfs_period_us` to 1000000.

  - To allow a process to utilize 100% of a single CPU, set `cpu.cfs_quota_us` to 1000000 and `cpu.cfs_period_us` to 1000000.

  - To allow a process to utilize 100% of two CPUs, set `cpu.cfs_quota_us` to 2000000 and `cpu.cfs_period_us` to 1000000.

To understand both of these control mechanisms, we can look into the aspects of the Linux CFS task scheduler. The aim of this scheduler is to grant a fair share of the CPU resources to all the tasks running on the system.

We can break up these tasks into two types:

- **CPU-intensive tasks**: Tasks like encryption, machine learning, query processing, and so on

- **I/O-intensive tasks**: Tasks that are using disk or network I/O like database clients

The scheduler has the responsibility of scheduling both kinds of tasks. The CFS uses a concept of `vruntime`. `vruntime` is a member of the `sched_entity` structure, which is a member of the `task_struct` structure (each process is represented in Linux by a `task_struct` structure):

```
struct task_struct {
    int prio, static_prio, normal_prio;
    unsigned int rt_priority;
    struct list_head run_list;
    const struct sched_class *sched_class;
    struct sched_entity se;
    unsigned int policy;
    cpumask_t cpus_allowed;
    unsigned int time_slice;
};
        }
struct sched_entity {
    /* For load-balancing: */
    struct load_weight          load;
    struct rb_node              run_node;
    struct list_head            group_node;
    unsigned int                on_rq;
    u64                         exec_start;
    u64                         sum_exec_runtime;
    u64                         vruntime;
    u64                         prev_sum_exec_runtime;
    u64                         nr_migrations;
    struct sched_statistics     statistics;
#ifdef CONFIG_FAIR_GROUP_SCHED
    Int                         depth;
    struct sched_entity         *parent;
    /* rq on which this entity is (to be) queued: */
    struct cfs_rq               *cfs_rq;
    /* rq "owned" by this entity/group: */
    struct cfs_rq               *my_q;
    /* cached value of my_q->h_nr_running */
    unsigned long               runnable_weight;
```

The task_struct structure has a reference to sched_entity, which holds a reference to vruntime.

vruntime is calculated using these steps:

1. Compute the time spent by the process on the CPU.

2. Weigh the computed running time against the number of runnable processes.

The kernel uses the update_curr function defined in the https:// elixir.bootlin.com/linux/latest/source/kernel/sched/fair.c file.

```c
/*
 * Update the current task's runtime statistics.
 */
static void update_curr(struct cfs_rq *cfs_rq)
{
    struct sched_entity *curr = cfs_rq->curr;
    u64 now = rq_clock_task(rq_of(cfs_rq));
    u64 delta_exec;

    if (unlikely(!curr))
        return;

    delta_exec = now - curr->exec_start;

    if (unlikely((s64)delta_exec <= 0))
        return;

    curr->exec_start = now;

    schedstat_set(curr->statistics.exec_max, max(delta_exec,
    curr->statistics.exec_max));
    curr->sum_exec_runtime += delta_exec;
    schedstat_add(cfs_rq->exec_clock, delta_exec);
    curr->vruntime += calc_delta_fair(delta_exec, curr);

    update_min_vruntime(cfs_rq);
```

```
if (entity_is_task(curr)) {
    struct task_struct *curtask = task_of(curr);
    trace_sched_stat_runtime(curtask, delta_exec, curr-
    >vruntime);
    cgroup_account_cputime(curtask, delta_exec);
    account_group_exec_runtime(curtask, delta_exec);
}

account_cfs_rq_runtime(cfs_rq, delta_exec);
}
```

The function first calculates the delta_exec, which is the time spent by the current task on the CPU. This delta_exec is then passed as a parameter to another function call, named calc_delta_fair. This call returns the weighted value of the process runtime in relation to the number of runnable processes. Once vruntime is calculated, it's stored as part of the sched_entity structure.

Also, as part of updating the vruntime for the task, the update_curr function calls update_min_vruntime. This calculates the smallest value of vruntime among all runnable processes and adds it to a red–black tree as the leftmost node. The CFS scheduler can then look into the red–black tree to schedule the process that has the lowest vruntime.

Basically, the CFS scheduler schedules its heuristic's schedules and I/O-intensive tasks more frequently, but gives more time to the CPU-intensive tasks in a single run. This also could be understood from the vruntime concept discussed previously. Since I/O tasks are mostly waiting for network/disk, their vruntimes values tend to be smaller than CPU tasks. That means the I/O tasks will be scheduled more frequently. The CPU-intensive tasks will get more time once they are scheduled to do the work. This way, CFS tries to attain a fair scheduling of tasks.

Let's pause for a minute and think about a potential problem this scheduling could lead to.

Assume you have two processes, A and B, belonging to different users. These processes each get 50% share of the CPU. Suppose a user owning process A launches another process, called A1. Now CFS will give a 33% share to each process. This effectively means that users of process A and A1 now get 66% of the CPU. A classic example is a database like PostgreSQL, which creates processes per connection. As number of connections grows, the number of processes grows. If fair scheduling is in place, each connection would tend to take away the share of the other non-Postgre processes running on the same machine.

This problem led to *group scheduling*. To understand this concept, let's look at another kernel data structure:

```
/* CFS-related fields in a runqueue */
struct cfs_rq {
    struct load_weight load;
    unsigned int nr_running;
    unsigned int h_nr_running;         /* SCHED_{NORMAL, BATCH,
                                          IDLE} */
    unsigned int idle_h_nr_running;  /* SCHED_IDLE */
    u64 exec_clock;
    u64 min_vruntime;

#ifndef CONFIG_64BIT
    u64 min_vruntime_copy;
#endif

    struct rb_root_cached tasks_timeline;
};
        /*
         * 'curr' points to currently running entity on
         this cfs_rq.
         * It is set to NULL otherwise (i.e. when none are
         currently running).
         */
```

```
struct sched_entity *curr;
struct sched_entity *next;
struct sched_entity *last;
struct sched_entity *skip;
```

This structure holds the number of runnable tasks in the nr_running member. The curr member is a pointer to the current running scheduling entity or the task.

Also, the sched_entity structure is now represented as a hierarchical data structure:

```
struct sched_entity {
/* For load-balancing: */
struct load_weight       load;
struct rb_node           run_node;
struct list_head         group_node;
unsigned int             on_rq;
u64                      exec_start;
u64                      sum_exec_runtime;
u64                      vruntime;
u64                      prev_sum_exec_runtime;
u64                      nr_migrations;
struct sched_statistics     statistics;
#ifdef CONFIG_FAIR_GROUP_SCHED
      Int                         depth;
      struct sched_entity     *parent;
      /* rq on which this entity is (to be) queued: */
      struct cfs_rq           *cfs_rq;
      /* rq "owned" by this entity/group: */
      struct cfs_rq           *my_q;
      /* cached value of my_q->h_nr_running */
      unsigned long           runnable_weight;
```

```
#endif
#ifdef CONFIG_SMP
        /*
         * Per entity load average tracking.
         *
         * Put into separate cache line so it does not
         * collide with read-mostly values above.
         */
            struct sched_avg avg;
#endif
};
```

This means there can now be `sched_entities` structures that are not associated with a process (`task_struct`). Instead, these entities can represent a group of processes. Each `sched_entity` now maintains a run queue of its own. A process can be moved to the child schedule entity, which means it will be part of the run queue that the child schedule entity has. This run queue can represent the processes in the group.

The code flow in the scheduler would do the following.

`Pick_next_entity` method is called to pick up the best candidate for scheduling. We assume that there is only one group running at this time. This means that the red–black tree associated with the `sched_entity` process is blank. The method now tries to get the child `sched_entity` of the current `sched_entity`. It checks the `cfs_rq`, which has the processes of the group enqueued. The process is scheduled.

The `vruntime` is based on the weights of the processes within the group. This allows us to do fair scheduling and prevent processes within a group from impacting the CPU usage of processes within other groups.

With the understanding that processes can be placed into groups, let's see how bandwidth enforcement can be applied to the group. Another data structure called `cfs_bandwidth`, defined in `sched.h`, plays a role:

```
struct cfs_bandwidth {
#ifdef CONFIG_CFS_BANDWIDTH
        raw_spinlock_t          lock;
        ktime_t                 period;
        u64                 quota;
        u64                 runtime;
        s64                 hierarchical_quota;
        u8                  idle;
        u8                  period_active;
        u8                  distribute_running;
        u8                  slack_started;
        struct hrtimer          period_timer;
        struct hrtimer          slack_timer;
        struct list_head    throttled_cfs_rq;
        /* Statistics: */
        Int                 nr_periods;
        Int                 nr_throttled;
        u64                 throttled_time;
#endif
};
```

This structure keeps track of the runtime quota for the group. The cff_bandwith_used function is used to return a Boolean value when the check is made in the account_cfs_rq_runtime method of the fair scheduler implementation file. If no runtime quota remains, the throttle_cfs_rq method is invoked. It dequeues the task from the run queue of the sched_entity and sets the throttled flag. The function implementation is shown here:

```
static void throttle_cfs_rq(struct cfs_rq *cfs_rq)
{
    struct rq *rq = rq_of(cfs_rq);
    struct cfs_bandwidth *cfs_b = tg_cfs_bandwidth(cfs_rq->tg);
```

```
struct sched_entity *se;
long task_delta, idle_task_delta, dequeue = 1;
bool empty;
se = cfs_rq->tg->se[cpu_of(rq_of(cfs_rq))];

/* Freeze hierarchy runnable averages while throttled */
rcu_read_lock();
walk_tg_tree_from(cfs_rq->tg, tg_throttle_down, tg_nop,
(void *)rq);
rcu_read_unlock();

task_delta = cfs_rq->h_nr_running;
idle_task_delta = cfs_rq->idle_h_nr_running;

for_each_sched_entity(se) {
    struct cfs_rq *qcfs_rq = cfs_rq_of(se);

    /* Throttled entity or throttle-on-deactivate */
    if (!se->on_rq)
        break;

    if (dequeue) {
        dequeue_entity(qcfs_rq, se, DEQUEUE_SLEEP);
    } else {
        update_load_avg(qcfs_rq, se, 0);
        se_update_runnable(se);
    }

    qcfs_rq->h_nr_running -= task_delta;
    qcfs_rq->idle_h_nr_running -= idle_task_delta;

    if (qcfs_rq->load.weight)
        dequeue = 0;
}
```

```
    if (!se)
        sub_nr_running(rq, task_delta);

    cfs_rq->throttled = 1;
    cfs_rq->throttled_clock = rq_clock(rq);

    raw_spin_lock(&cfs_b->lock);
    empty = list_empty(&cfs_b->throttled_cfs_rq);

    /*
     * Add to the _head_ of the list, so that an
     already-started
     * distribute_cfs_runtime will not see us. If distribute_
     cfs_runtime is
     * not running, add to the tail so that later runqueues
     don't get starved.
     */
    if (cfs_b->distribute_running)
        list_add_rcu(&cfs_rq->throttled_list, &cfs_b-
        >throttled_cfs_rq);
    else
        list_add_tail_rcu(&cfs_rq->throttled_list, &cfs_b-
        >throttled_cfs_rq);

    /*
     * If we're the first throttled task, make sure the
     bandwidth
     * timer is running.
     */
    if (empty)
        start_cfs_bandwidth(cfs_b);

    raw_spin_unlock(&cfs_b->lock);
}
```

This explains how the CPU cgroups allow tasks/processes to be grouped and can use the CPU shares mechanism to enforce fair scheduling within a group. This also explains how quota and bandwidth enforcement is accomplished within a group. We now discuss the other cgroup type, which enforces resource limits on block I/O.

Block I/O Cgroups

The purpose of the block I/O cgroup is twofold:

- **Provides fairness to the individual cgroup**: Makes use of a scheduler called complete fair queuing

- **Does block I/O throttling**: Enforces a quota on the block I/O (bytes as well as iops) per cgroup

Before delving into details of how the cgroup for block I/O is implemented, we'll take a small detour to investigate how the Linux block I/O works. Figure 4-1 is a high-level block diagram of how the block I/O request flows through the user space to the device.

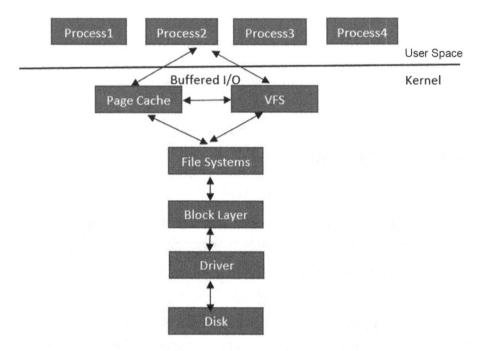

Figure 4-1. *The block I/O request flows through the user space to the device*

The application issues a read/write request either via the file system or via memory-mapped files. In either case, the request hits the page cache (kernel buffer for caching file data). With a file system–based call, the virtual file system (VFS) handles the system call and invokes the underlying registered file system.

The next layer is the block layer where the actual I/O request is constructed. There are three important data structures within the block layer:

- request_queue: A single queue architecture is where there is one request queue per device. This is the queue where the block layer, in tandem with the I/O scheduler, queues the request. The device driver drains the request queue and submits the request to the actual device.

- request: The request structure represents the single I/O request to be delivered to the I/O device. The request is made of a list of bio structures.

- **bio**: The bio structure is the basic container for block I/O. Within the kernel is the bio structure. Defined in <linux/bio.h>, this structure represents block I/O operations that are in flight (active) as a list of segments. A segment is a chunk of a buffer that is contiguous in memory.

Diagrammatically, the bio structure is shown in Figure 4-2.

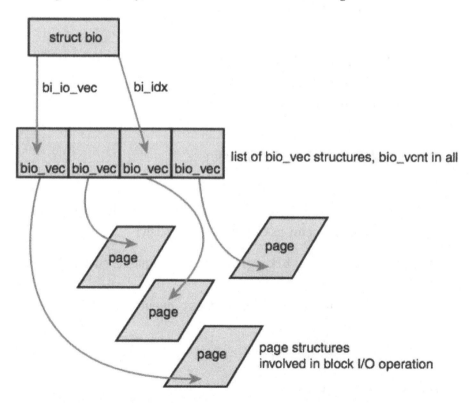

Figure 4-2. *The* bio *structure represents block I/O operations that are in flight (active) as a list of segments*

bio_vec represents a specific segment and has a pointer to the page holding the block data at a specific offset.

The requests are submitted to the request queue and drained by the device driver. The important data structures involved in implementing the block I/O cgroup within the Linux kernel are shown here:

```
struct blkcg {
    struct cgroup_subsys_state css;
    spinlock_t lock;
    struct radix_tree_root blkg_tree;
    struct blkcg_gq __rcu *blkg_hint;
    struct hlist_head blkg_list;
    struct blkcg_policy_data *cpd[BLKCG_MAX_POLS];

#ifdef CONFIG_CGROUP_WRITEBACK
    struct list_head cgwb_list;
    refcount_t cgwb_refcnt;
#endif

    struct list_head all_blkcgs_node;
};
```

This structure represents the block I/O cgroup. Each block I/O cgroup is mapped to a request queue, as explained previously:

```
/* association between a blk cgroup and a request queue */
struct blkcg_gq {
    /* Pointer to the associated request_queue */
    struct request_queue *q;
    struct list_head q_node;
    struct hlist_node blkcg_node;
    struct blkcg *blkcg;

    /*
```

```
* Each blkg gets congested separately, and the congestion
state is
* propagated to the matching bdi_writeback_congested.
*/
struct bdi_writeback_congested *wb_congested;

/* All non-root blkcg_gq's are guaranteed to have access to
parent */
struct blkcg_gq *parent;

/* Request allocation list for this blkcg-q pair */
struct request_list rl;

/* Reference count */
atomic_t refcnt;

/* Is this blkg online? Protected by both blkcg and q
locks */
bool online;

struct blkg_rwstat stat_bytes;
struct blkg_rwstat stat_ios;
struct blkg_policy_data *pd[BLKCG_MAX_POLS];

struct rcu_head rcu_head;
atomic_t use_delay;
atomic64_t delay_nsec;
atomic64_t delay_start;
u64 last_delay;
int last_use;
};
```

Each request queue is associated with a block I/O cgroup.

Understanding Fairness

Fairness in this context means that each cgroup should get a fair share of the I/O issued to the device. To accomplish this, a CFQ (Complete Fair Queuing) scheduler must be configured. Without cgroups in place, the CFQ scheduler assigns each process a queue and then gives a time slice to each queue, thereby handling fairness.

A *service tree* is a list of active queues/processes on which the scheduler runs. So basically, the CFQ scheduler services requests from the queues on the service tree.

With cgroups in place, the concept of a *CFQ group* is introduced. Now, instead of scheduling per process, the scheduling happens at the group level. This means each cgroup has multiple service trees on which the group queues are scheduled. Then there is a global service tree on which the CFQ groups are scheduled.

The CFQ group structure is defined as follows:

```
struct cfq_group {
    /* must be the first member */
    struct blkg_policy_data pd;
    /* group service_tree member */
    struct rb_node rb_node;
    /* group service_tree key */
u64 vdisktime;
    /*
    * The number of active cfqgs and sum of their weights
    under this
    * cfqg. This covers this cfqg's leaf_weight and all children's
    * weights, but does not cover weights of further descendants.
    *
```

```
 * If a cfqg is on the service tree, it's active. An active cfqg
 * also activates its parent and contributes to the children_weight
 * of the parent.
 */
int nr_active;
unsigned int children_weight;
 /*
 * vfraction is the fraction of vdisktime that the tasks in this
 * cfqg are entitled to. This is determined by compounding the
 * ratios walking up from this cfqg to the root.
 *
 * It is in fixed point w/ CFQ_SERVICE_SHIFT and the sum of all
 * vfractions on a service tree is approximately 1. The sum may
 * deviate a bit due to rounding errors and fluctuations caused by
 * cfqgs entering and leaving the service tree.
 */
 * unsigned int vfraction;
 /*
 * There are two weights - (internal) weight is the weight of this
 * cfqg against the sibling cfqgs. leaf_weight is the weight of
 * this cfqg against the child cfqgs. For the root cfqg, both
 * weights are kept in sync for backward compatibility.
 */
unsigned int weight;
unsigned int new_weight;
unsigned int dev_weight;
unsigned int leaf_weight;
unsigned int new_leaf_weight;
```

```
unsigned int dev_leaf_weight;
/* number of cfqq currently on this group */
int nr_cfqq;
/*
 * Per group busy queues average. Useful for workload
 slice calc.
 * We create the array for each prio class but at runtime
 it is used
 * only for RT and BE class and slot for IDLE class
 remains unused.
 * This is primarily done to avoid confusion and a gcc
 warning.
 */
unsigned int
busy_queues_avg[CFQ_PRIO_NR]; /*
 *rr lists of queues with requests. We maintain service
 trees for
 *RT and BE classes. These trees are subdivided in subclasses
 * of SYNC, SYNC_NOIDLE and ASYNC based on workload type. For
 * the IDLE class there is no subclassification and all the
 CFQ queues go on
 * a single tree service_tree_idle.
 * Counts are embedded in the cfq_rb_root
 */
struct cfq_rb_root service_trees[2][3];
struct cfq_rb_root service_tree_idle;
u64 saved_wl_slice;
enum wl_type_t saved_wl_type;
enum wl_class_t saved_wl_class;
  /* number of requests that are on the dispatch list or
  inside driver */
int dispatched;
```

```
    struct cfq_ttime ttime;
    struct cfqg_stats stats;          /* stats for this cfqg */
    /* async queue for each priority case */ struct
    cfq_queue *async_cfqq[2][IOPRIO_BE_NR]; struct
    cfq_queue *async_idle_cfqq;
};
```

Each CFQ group contains an "io weight" value that can be configured in cgroup. The CFQG's (CFQ groups) vdisktime decides its position on the "cfqg service tree," and then it's charged according to the "io weight".

Understanding Throttling

Throttling provides a means to apply resource limits to the block I/O. This enables the kernel to control the max block I/O that a user-space process can get. The kernel realizes this via the block I/O cgroup.

Throttling the block I/O per cgroup is done using a set of different functions. The first function is blk_throttl_bio and it's defined in blk-throttle.c (see https://elixir.bootlin.com/linux/latest/source/block/blk-throttle.c):

```
bool blk_throtl_bio(struct request_queue *q, struct blkcg_gq
*blkg, struct bio *bio)
{
    struct throtl_qnode *qn = NULL;
    struct throtl_grp *tg = blkg_to_tg(blkg ?: q->root_blkg);
    struct throtl_service_queue *sq;
    bool rw = bio_data_dir(bio);
    bool throttled = false;
    struct throtl_data *td = tg->td;

    WARN_ON_ONCE(!rcu_read_lock_held());
```

```
    /* See throtl_charge_bio() */
    if (bio_flagged(bio, BIO_THROTTLED) || !tg->has_rules[rw])
        goto out;

    spin_lock_irq(q->queue_lock);
    throtl_update_latency_buckets(td);

    if (unlikely(blk_queue_bypass(q)))
        goto out_unlock;

    blk_throtl_assoc_bio(tg, bio);
    blk_throtl_update_idletime(tg);
    sq = &tg->service_queue;

again:
    while (true) {
        if (tg->last_low_overflow_time[rw] == 0)
            tg->last_low_overflow_time[rw] = jiffies;

        throtl_downgrade_check(tg);
        throtl_upgrade_check(tg);

        /* Throtl is FIFO - if bios are already queued, we
        should queue */
        if (sq->nr_queued[rw])
            break;

        /* If above limits, break to queue */
        if (!tg_may_dispatch(tg, bio, NULL)) {
            tg->last_low_overflow_time[rw] = jiffies;

            if (throtl_can_upgrade(td, tg)) {
                throtl_upgrade_state(td);
                goto again;
            }
```

```
    break;
}
/* Within limits, let's charge and dispatch directly */
throtl_charge_bio(tg, bio);

/*
 * We need to trim slice even when bios are not
being queued
 * otherwise it might happen that a bio is not
queued for
 * a long time and slice keeps on extending, and
trim is not
 * called for a long time. Now if limits are reduced
suddenly
 * we take into account all the IO dispatched so far
at the new
 * low rate and newly queued IO gets a really long
dispatch time.
 *
 * So keep on trimming slice even if bio is not queued.
 */
throtl_trim_slice(tg, rw);

/*
 * @bio passed through this layer without being
throttled.
 * Climb up the ladder. If we're already at the top, it
 * can be executed directly.
 **/
qn = &tg->qnode_on_parent[rw];
sq = sq->parent_sq;
tg = sq_to_tg(sq);
```

```
    if (!tg)
        goto out_unlock;
}

/* Out-of-limit, queue to @tg */
throtl_log(sq, "[%c] bio. bdisp=%llu sz=%u bps=%llu
iodisp=%u iops=%u queued=%d/%d",
            rw == READ ? 'R' : 'W',
            tg->bytes_disp[rw], bio->bi_iter.bi_size,
            tg_bps_limit(tg, rw),
            tg->io_disp[rw], tg_iops_limit(tg, rw),
            sq->nr_queued[READ], sq->nr_queued[WRITE]);

tg->last_low_overflow_time[rw] = jiffies;
td->nr_queued[rw]++;
throtl_add_bio_tg(bio, qn, tg);
throttled = true;

/*
 * Update @tg's dispatch time and force schedule
 dispatch if @tg
 * was empty before @bio. The forced scheduling isn't
 likely to
 * cause undue delay as @bio is likely to be dispatched
 directly if
 * @tg's disptime is not in the future.
 */
if (tg->flags & THROTL_TG_WAS_EMPTY) {
    tg_update_disptime(tg);
    throtl_schedule_next_dispatch(tg->service_queue.parent_
    sq, true);
}
```

```
out_unlock:
    spin_unlock_irq(q->queue_lock);

out:
    bio_set_flag(bio, BIO_THROTTLED);

#ifdef CONFIG_BLK_DEV_THROTTLING_LOW
    if (throttled || !td->track_bio_latency)
        bio->bi_issue.value |= BIO_ISSUE_THROTL_SKIP_LATENCY;
#endif

    return throttled;
}
```

The following code snippet checks if the bio can be dispatched to be pushed to the device driver:

```
if (!tg_may_dispatch(tg, bio, NULL)) { tg-
            >last_low_overflow_time[rw] = jiffies;
        if (throtl_can_upgrade(td, tg)) {
                throtl_upgrade_state(td);
            goto again;
        }
        break;
}
```

The tg_may_dispatch definition is shown here:

```
static bool tg_may_dispatch(struct throtl_grp *tg, struct
bio  *bio, unsigned long *wait)
{
    bool rw = bio_data_dir(bio);
    unsigned long bps_wait = 0, iops_wait = 0, max_wait = 0;
    /*
```

```
 * Currently the whole state machine of group depends on
first bio
 * queued in the group bio list. So one should not be calling
 * this function with a different bio if there are other bios
 * queued.
 * /
BUG_ON(tg->service_queue.nr_queued[rw] &&
  bio != throtl_peek_queued(&tg->service_queue.queued[rw]));
/* If tg->bps = -1, then BW is unlimited */
   if (tg_bps_limit(tg, rw) == U64_MAX &&
       tg_iops_limit(tg, rw) == UINT_MAX) {
     if (wait)
          *wait = 0;
     return true;
  }
 /*
 * If the previous slice expired, start a new one, otherwise
 * renew/extend the existing slice to make sure it is at
least throtl_slice interval
 * long since now. The new slice is started only for empty
throttle
 * group. If there is queued bio, that means there
should be an
 * active slice and it should be extended instead.
 * /
if (throtl_slice_used(tg, rw) &&
   !(tg->service_queue.nr_queued[rw]))
      throtl_start_new_slice(tg, rw);
   else {
       if (time_before(tg->slice_end[rw],
           jiffies + tg->td->throtl_slice))
```

```
            throtl_extend_slice(tg, rw,
                jiffies + tg->td->throtl_slice);
    }
    if (tg_with_in_bps_limit(tg, bio, &bps_wait) &&
        tg_with_in_iops_limit(tg, bio, &iops_wait)) {
        if (wait)
            *wait = 0;
        return true;
    }
    max_wait = max(bps_wait, iops_wait);
    if (wait)
            *wait = max_wait;
    if (time_before(tg->slice_end[rw], jiffies + max_wait))
        throtl_extend_slice(tg, rw, jiffies + max_wait);
    return false;
    The snippet
    if (tg_with_in_bps_limit(tg, bio, &bps_wait) &&
        tg_with_in_iops_limit(tg, bio, &iops_wait)) {
        if (wait)
            *wait = 0;
        return true;
}
```

This determines if the bio is within the limits for that cgroup or not. As evident, it checks both the bytes per sec limit and the I/O per sec limit for the cgroup.

If the limit is not exceeded, the bio is first charged to the cgroup:

```
/* within limits, let's charge and dispatch directly */ throtl_
charge_bio(tg, bio);
static void throtl_charge_bio(struct throtl_grp *tg, struct
bio *bio) {
    bool rw = bio_data_dir(bio);
```

```
unsigned int bio_size =
                        throtl_bio_data_size (bio);
/* Charge the bio to the group */
tg->bytes_disp[rw] += bio_size;
tg->io_disp[rw]++;
tg->last_bytes_disp[rw] += bio_size;
tg->last_io_disp[rw]++;
 /*
* BIO_THROTTLED is used to prevent the same bio to be
throttled
* more than once as a throttled bio will go through blk-
throtl the
* second time when it eventually gets issued.  Set it
when a bio
* is being charged to a tg.
*/
 if (!bio_flagged(bio, BIO_THROTTLED))
     bio_set_flag(bio, BIO_THROTTLED);
 }
```

This function charges the bio (the bytes and iops) to the throttle group. It then passes the bio up to the parent, as evident in the following code:

```
/*
    * @bio passed through this layer without being throttled.
    * Climb up the ladder.  If we're already at the top, it
    * can be executed directly.
    */
    qn = &tg->qnode_on_parent[rw];
    sq = sq->parent_sq;
    tg = sq_to_tg(sq);
```

If the limits are exceeded, the code takes a different flow. The following code snippet is called:

```
throtl_add_bio_tg(bio, qn, tg);
throttled = true;
```

Let's look at the throtl_add_bio_tg function in more detail:

```
/**
 * throtl_add_bio_tg - add a bio to the specified throtl_grp
 * @bio: bio to add
 * @qn: qnode to use
 * @tg: the target throtl_grp
 *
 Add @bio to @tg's service_queue using @qn. If @qn is not
 specified,
 tg->qnode_on_self[] is used.
 */
static void throtl_add_bio_tg(struct bio *bio, struct
throtl_qnode *qn,
            struct throtl_grp *tg)
{
    struct throtl_service_queue *sq = &tg-
    >service_queue; bool rw = bio_data_dir(bio);
    if (!qn)
        qn = &tg->qnode_on_self[rw];
    /*
    * If @tg doesn't currently have any bios queued in
    the same
    * direction, queueing @bio can change when @tg should be
    * dispatched.  Mark that @tg was empty.  This is
    automatically
    * cleared on the next tg_update_disptime().
```

```
*/
if (!sq->nr_queued[rw])
    tg->flags |= THROTL_TG_WAS_EMPTY;
throtl_qnode_add_bio(bio, qn, &sq->queued[rw]);
sq->nr_queued[rw]++;
throtl_enqueue_tg(tg);
}
```

This function adds the bio to the throttle service queue. This queue acts as a mechanism to throttle the bio requests. The service request is then drained later:

```
/**
  *blk_throtl_drain - drain throttled bios
  *@q: request_queue to drain throttled bios for
  *Dispatch all currently throttled bios on @q through
  - >make_request_fn().
  */
void blk_throtl_drain(struct request_queue *q)
__releases(q->queue_lock) __acquires(q->queue_lock)
{
struct throtl_data *td = q-
>td; struct blkcg_gq *blkg;
struct cgroup_subsys_state *pos_css;
struct bio *bio;
int rw;
queue_lockdep_assert_held(q);
rcu_read_lock();
  /*
  * Drain each tg while doing post-order walk on the blkg
  tree, so
```

```
 * that all bios are propagated to td->service_
 queue.  It'd be
 * better to walk service_queue tree directly but
 blkg walk is
 * easier.
 */
blkg_for_each_descendant_post(blkg, pos_css, td->queue-
>root_blkg)
   tg_drain_bios(&blkg_to_tg(blkg)->service_queue);
 /* finally, transfer bios from top-level tg's into
 the td */
 tg_drain_bios(&td->service_queue);
 rcu_read_unlock();
 spin_unlock_irq(q->queue_lock);
/* all bios now should be in td->service_queue, issue them
*/ for (rw = READ; rw <= WRITE; rw++)
       while ((bio = throtl_pop_queued(&td-
>service_queue.queued[rw],
                               NULL)))
               generic_make_request(bio);
 spin_lock_irq(q->queue_lock);
```

Summary

In this chapter we looked at how resources for a tenant can be constrained using a mechanism in the Linux kernel called cgroups. We covered various data structures within the Linux kernel that enable the cgroups. We also examined some code examples showing how cgroups can be enabled from user-space applications.

CHAPTER 5

Layered File Systems

In Chapters 3 and 4, we addressed the topics of process isolation via
Linux namespaces and resource control for individual processes via
cgroups, respectively. Now we delve into the topic of layered file systems,
which constitute the third building block of the Linux container, after
namespaces and cgroups. This chapter describes how layered files systems
enable file sharing on the host and how this helps in running multiple
containers on the host.

Let's start by discussing what a file system is.

A File System Primer

The Linux philosophy is to treat everything as a file. As an example, socket,
pipe, and block devices are all represented as files in Linux.

The file systems in Linux act as containers to abstract the underlying
storage in the case of block devices. For non-block devices like sockets and
pipes, there are file systems in memory that have operations that can be
invoked using the standard file system API.

© Shashank Mohan Jain 2023
S. M. Jain, *Linux Containers and Virtualization*,
https://doi.org/10.1007/978-1-4842-9768-1_5

Linux abstracts all file systems using a layer called the virtual file system (VFS). All file systems register with the VFS. The VFS has the following important data structures:

- **File**: This represents the open file and captures the information, like offset, and so on. The user space has a handle to an opened file via a structure called the *file descriptor*. This is the handle used to interface with the file system.

- **Inode**: This is mapped 1:1 to the file. The *inode* is one of the most critical structures and holds the metadata about the file. As an example, it includes in which data blocks the file data is stored and which access permissions are on the file. This info is part of the inode. Inodes are also stored on disk by the specific file system, but there is a representation in memory that's part of the VFS layer. The file system is responsible for enumerating the VFS inode structure.

- **Dentry**: This is the mapping between the filename and inode. This is an in-memory structure and is not stored on disk. This is mainly relevant to lookup and path traversal.

- **Superblock**: This structure holds all the information about the file system, including how many blocks are there, the device name, and so on. This structure is enumerated and brought into memory during a mount operation.

Each of these data structures holds pointers to their specific operations. As an example, *file* has file_ops for reading and writing and *superblock* has operations via super_ops to mount, unmount, and so on.

The mount operation creates a vfsmount data structure, which holds a reference to a new superblock structure created from the file system to be mounted on the disk. The dentry has a reference to the vfsmount. This is where the VFS distinguishes between a directory and a mount point. During a traversal, if the vfsmount is found in a dentry, the inode number 2 on the mounted device is used (inode 2 is reserved for the root directory).

So how does this all fit together in the case of a block device? Say that the user-space process makes a call to read a file. The system call is made to the kernel. The VFS checks the path and determines if there are dentries cached from the root. As it traverses and finds the right dentry, it locates the inode for the file to be opened. Once the inode is located, the permissions are checked and the data blocks are loaded from the disk into the OS page cache. The same data is moved into the user space of the process.

The page cache is an interesting optimization in the OS. All reads and writes (except direct I/O) happen over the page cache. The page cache itself is represented by a data structure called address_space. This address_space holds a tree of memory pages, and the file inode holds a reference to that address_space data structure.

Figure 5-1 shows how a file maps into the page cache. This is also the key to understanding how operations like mmap for memory-mapped files work.

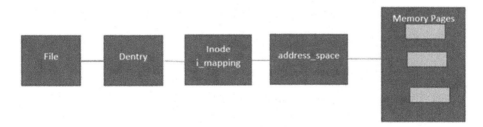

Figure 5-1. Mapping a file to a page cache

If the file read request is in the page cache (which is determined via the address_space structure of the file's inode), the data is served from there.

Whenever a write call is made on the file via the file descriptor, the writes are first written to the page cache. The memory pages are marked dirty and the Linux kernel uses the write-back cache mechanism, which means there are threads in the background (called pdflush) that drain the page cache and write to the physical disk via the block driver. The mechanism of marking pages dirty doesn't happen at the page level. Pages can be 4KB in size and even a minimal change will then cause a full page write.

To avoid that, there are structures that have more fine-grained granularity and represent a disk block in memory. These structures are called *buffer heads*. For example, if the block size is 512 bytes, there are eight buffer heads and one page in the page cache. That way, individual blocks can be marked dirty and made part of the writes.

The buffers can be explicitly flushed to disk via these system calls:

- sync(): Flushes all dirty buffers to disk.

- fsync(fd): Flushes only the file-specific dirty buffers to disk, including the changes to inode.

- fdatasync(fd): Flushes only the dirty data buffers of the file to disk. Doesn't flush the inodes.

Here's an example of how this sync process works:

1. Check if the superblock is dirty.

2. Write back the superblock.

3. Iterate over each inode from the inode list:

    a. If the inode is dirty, write it back.

    b. If the page cache of the inode is dirty, write it back.

    c. Clear the dirty flag.

Figure 5-2 shows the file system's different layers under the kernel.

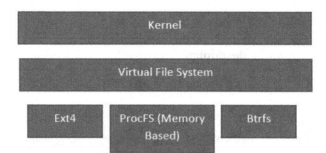

Figure 5-2. *The different layers of a file system under the kernel*

Examples of different kinds of file systems include:

- **Ext4**: This file system is used to access the underlying block devices.

- **ProcFS**: This is an in-memory file system and is used to provide features. This is also called a *pseudo file system*.

Brief Overview of Pseudo File Systems

Recall that the general philosophy of Linux is that everything is a file. Working on that premise, pseudo file systems expose some of the kernel's resources over the file interface. One such file system is procfs.

The procfs file system is mounted on the rootfs under the proc directory. The data under procfs is not persisted and all operations happen in memory.

Some of the structures exposed via procfs are explained in the following table:

Structure	Description
/proc/cpuinfo	CPU details like cores, CPU size, make, etc.
/proc/meminfo	Information about physical memory.
/proc/interrupts	Information about interrupts and handlers.
/proc/vmstat	Virtual memory stats.
/proc/filesystems	Active file systems on the kernel.
/proc/mounts	Current mounts and devices; this will be specific to the mount namespace.
/proc/uptime	Time since the kernel was up.
/proc/stat	System statistics.
/proc/net	Network-related structures like TCP sockets, files, etc. proc also exposes some process-specific information via files.
/proc/pid/cmdline	Command-line name of the process.
/proc/pid/environ	Environment variables of the process.
/proc/pid/mem	Virtual memory of the process.
/proc/pid/maps	Mapping of the virtual memory.
/proc/pid/fdinfo	Open file descriptors of the process.
/proc/pid/task	Details of the child processes.

Understanding layered File Systems

Now that you have a better understanding of the file systems in Linux, it's time to take a look at the layered file systems in Linux.

A layered file system allows files to be shared on disk, thereby saving space. Since these files are shared in memory (loaded in page cache), a layered file system allows optimal space utilization as well as faster bootup.

Consider an example of running ten Cassandra databases on the same host, each database running its own namespaces. If we have separate file systems for each database's different inodes, we don't enjoy these advantages:

- Memory sharing

- Sharing on disk

By contrast, a layered file system is broken into layers and each layer is a read-only file system. Since these layers are shared across the containers on the same host, they tend to use storage optimally. And, since the inodes are the same, they refer to the same OS page cache. This makes things optimal from all aspects.

Compare this to VM-based provisioning, where each rootfs is provisioned as a disk. This means they all have different inode representations on the host and there is no optimal storage as compared to the containers.

Hypervisors also tend to reach optimization using techniques like KSM (Kernel Same Page Merging) so they can deduplicate across VMs for the same pages.

Next, we discuss the concept of union file systems, which is a type of layered file system.

The Union File System

According to Wikipedia, the union file system is a file system service for Linux, FreeBSD, and NetBSD that implements a union mount for other file systems. It allows files and directories of separate file systems, known as *branches*, to be transparently overlaid, forming a single coherent file system. The contents of any directories that have the same path within the merged branches will be seen together in a single merged directory, within the new virtual file system.

So, basically, a union file system allows you to take different file systems and create a union of their contents, with the top layer providing a view of all the files underlying it. If duplicate files are found, the top layer supersedes the layers below it.

OverlayFS

This section looks at OverlayFS as one example of a union file system. OverlayFS has been part of the Linux Kernel since 3.18. It overlays (as the name suggests) the contents of one directory onto other. The source directories can be on different disks or file systems.

With OverlayFS v1, there were only two layers, and they were used to create a unified layer, as shown in Figure 5-3.

Figure 5-3. OverlayFS v1 with two layers (upper and lower)

OverlayFS v2 has three layers:

- **Base**: This is the base layer. This is primarily read-only.

- **Overlay**: This layer provides visibility from the base layer and allows users to add new files/directories. If any files from the base layer change, they are stored in the next layer.

- **Diff**: The changes made in the overlay layer are stored in the diff layer. Any changes to files in the base layer lead to copying the file from the base layer to the diff layer. The changes are then written in the diff layer.

Let's look at an example of how OverlayFS v2 works:

```
root@instance-1:~# mkdir base diff overlay workdir
root@instance-1:~# echo "test data" > base/test1
root@instance-1:~# sudo mount \
>       -t overlay \
>       -o lowerdir=base,upperdir=diff,workdir=workdir \
>       overlay \
>       overlay
root@instance-1:~# 
```

We create a file in the overlay directory and can see that it appears in diff:

```
root@instance-1:~/overlay# touch test2
root@instance-1:~/overlay# ls
test1  test2
root@instance-1:~/overlay# cd ../dif
-bash: cd: ../dif: No such file or directory
root@instance-1:~/overlay# cd ../diff
root@instance-1:~/diff# ls
test2
```

We now modify the test1 file:

```
root@instance-1:~/diff# nano test1
root@instance-1:~/diff# cd ../overlay/
root@instance-1:~/overlay# nano test1
root@instance-1:~/overlay# cat test1
test data
. Modifying
root@instance-1:~/overlay# cd ../base
root@instance-1:~/base# cat test1
test data
root@instance-1:~/base# █
```

If we check the file in the diff directory, we see the changed file. However, if we go to the base directory, we still see the old file. This means that when we modified the file in the base directory, it was copied to the diff directory first, after which the changes were made.

After these examples are executed, if users wanted to do a cleanup of resources, they could execute the following command to unmount the OverlayFS:

```
root@instance-1: umount overlay
```

After the unmount is complete, the directories can also be removed if desired.

Let's now consider how container engines like Docker implement this process. There is an Overlay2 storage driver in Docker, which you can find out more about at https://github.com/moby/moby/blob/master/daemon/graphdriver/overlay2/overlay.go.

Docker creates multiple read layers (base layers) and one read/write layer called the container layer (in our case, the overlay layer).

The multiple read layers can be shared across different containers on the same host, thereby attaining very high optimization. As hinted at earlier, since we have the same file system and the same inodes, the OS page cache is also shared across all containers on the same host.

Contrary to this, if we see a Docker driver device mapper, since it gives a virtual disk for each layer, we might not experience the sharing we get with OverlayFS. But now, even with the device mapper usage in Docker, we can pass the `-shared-rootfs` option to the daemon to share the `rootfs`. This basically works by creating a device for the first container base image and then doing bind mounts for subsequent containers. The bind mounts allow us to preserve the same inodes, and therefore the page cache is shared.

Summary

This chapter provided a comprehensive overview of file systems, including the concept of layered file systems with a focus on OverlayFS. It explained how Linux treats everything as a file and uses the virtual file system to abstract various file systems. The VFS employs essential data structures like File, Inode, Dentry, and Superblock to manage file operations efficiently. It details how the page cache optimizes read and write operations by caching recently accessed data in memory. The chapter then explored the advantages of layered file systems, where multiple read-only layers can be combined, enabling files to be shared and efficiently managed. It also discussed how container engines like Docker utilize OverlayFS to optimize storage and facilitate shared inodes, leading to a more efficient use of the OS page cache.

CHAPTER 6

Creating a Simple Container Framework

In the previous chapters, you learned about the important building blocks of the container framework: namespaces, cgroups, and layered file systems. In this chapter, you learn how these building blocks make up the container framework by building your own simple container framework.

Since we have covered the basics of what constitutes a container, it is time to look at how to write your own simple container. By the end of this chapter, you will have created your own simple container using namespace isolation.

Let's get started.

I have tested the commands that appear in the chapter on Ubuntu 19.04 with Linux Kernel 5.0.0-13.

The UTS Namespace

The first command we explore is called unshare. This command allows you to unshare a set of namespaces from the host. We will enter a new uts namespace and change the hostname within that namespace:

```
root@osboxes:~# unshare -u /bin/bash
root@osboxes:~# hostname test
```

© Shashank Mohan Jain 2023
S. M. Jain, *Linux Containers and Virtualization*,
https://doi.org/10.1007/978-1-4842-9768-1_6

```
root@osboxes:~# hostname
test
root@osboxes:~# exit
exit
root@osboxes:~# hostname
osboxes
```

After entering the UTS namespace, we changed the hostname to test, and this is what is reflected within that namespace. Once we exit and reenter the host namespace, we get the host namespace.

The command unshare -u /bin/bash creates the uts namespace and executes our process (/bin/bash) within that namespace. Note that if we don't change the hostname after entering the namespace, we still get the hostname of the host. This is not desirable, as we need a way to set this before executing our program within the namespace.

This is where we will explore writing a container using Go (also called Golang) and then set up namespaces before we launch the process within the container. Golang is the most common systems programming language around. It is used to create container runtimes like Docker, as well as container orchestration engines like Swarm and Kubernetes. Apart from that, it has been used in various other systems programming settings. It's a good idea to have a decent understanding of Golang before you delve into the code in this chapter.

Naturally, writing the container in Golang first requires installing Golang on the VM or on the machine on which you are working, as described next. (For complete instructions on Golang download and installation, visit https://go.dev/doc/install.)

Golang Installation

Here are the quick Golang install commands:

```
root@osboxes:~# wget https://go.dev/dl/go1.20.6.linux-
amd64.tar.gz
root@osboxes:~# tar -C /usr/local -xzf go1.20.6.linux-
amd64.tar.gz
```

You can add the following line to /root/.profile to add the Golang binaries to the system PATH variable:

```
root@osboxes:~# export PATH=$PATH:/usr/local/go/bin
```

Then run this command in your terminal:

```
root@osboxes:~# source ~/.profile
```

To check if Go (Golang) is installed properly, you can run this command:

```
root@osboxes:~# go version
```

If the installation was successful, you should see the following output:

```
root@instance-1:/home/jain_sm# go version
go version go1.20.6 linux/amd64
```

Now we will build a container with only a namespace and then keep modifying the program to add more functionalities, like shell support, rootfs, networking, and cgroups.

Building a Container with a Namespace

Let's revisit Linux namespaces briefly before we build the container. Namespaces are in the Linux kernel, similar to sandbox kernel resources like file systems, process trees, message queues, and semaphores, as well as network components like devices, sockets, and routing rules.

Namespaces isolate processes within their own execution sandbox so that they run completely isolated from other processes in different namespaces.

There are six namespaces which are covered here namely PID, Mount, UTS, Network, IPC and User namespaces:

- **PID**: The processes within the PID namespace have a different process tree. They have an init process with a PID of 1.

- **Mount**: This namespace controls which mount points a process can see. If a process is within a namespace, it will only see the mounts within that namespace.

- **UTS**: This allows a process to see a different namespace than the actual global namespace.

- **Network**: This namespace gives a different network view within a namespace. Network constructs like ports, iptables, and so on, are scoped within the namespace.

- **IPC**: This namespace confines interprocess communication structures like pipes within a specific namespace.

- **User**: This namespace allows for a separate user and group view within the namespace.

We don't discuss the cgroup namespace here, which (as described in Chapter 3) also allows the cgroups to be scoped into their own namespaces.

Now let's get our hands dirty and create a Go class called myuts.go. Copy the following snippet and use go build myuts.go to get the myuts binary. Also execute the **myuts** binary as the root user.

```go
package main
import (
 "fmt"
 "os"
 "os/exec"
 "syscall"
)
func main() {
 cmd := exec.Command("/bin/bash")
 // The statements below refer to the input, output and error
 streams of the process created (cmd)
 cmd.Stdin = os.Stdin
 cmd.Stdout = os.Stdout
 cmd.Stderr = os.Stderr
 //setting an environment variable
 cmd.Env = []string{"name=shashank"}
 // the command below creates a UTS namespace for the process
    cmd.SysProcAttr = &syscall.SysProcAttr{
        Cloneflags: syscall.CLONE_NEWUTS,
    }
 if err := cmd.Run(); err != nil {
    fmt.Printf("Error running the /bin/bash command -
    %s\n", err)
    os.Exit(1)
 }
}
```

This is a simple Go program that executes a shell, sets up the I/O streams for the process, and then sets one env variable. Then it uses the following command to create a UTS namespace:

```
cmd.SysProcAttr = &syscall.SysProcAttr{
    Cloneflags: syscall.CLONE_NEWUTS,
}
```

It then passes the CLONE flags (in this case, we just pass UTS as the Clone flag). The clone flags control which namespaces are created for the process.

After that, we build and run this Golang process. We can see whether the new namespace was created by using the proc file system and checking the proc/<<pid>>/ns:

```
root@osboxes:~/book_prep# ls -li /proc/self/ns/uts
15738 lrwxrwxrwx 1 root root 0 Jul 13 15:53 /proc/self/ns/uts
-> 'uts:[4026531838]'

root@osboxes:~/book_prep# ./myuts
root@osboxes:/root/book_prep# ls -li /proc/self/ns/uts
17043 lrwxrwxrwx 1 root root 0 Jul 13 16:06 /proc/self/ns/uts
-> 'uts:[4026532325]'
root@osboxes:/root/book_prep#exit
```

First, we print the namespace of the host and then we print the namespace of the container we are in.

We can see that the uts namespaces are different.

Adding More Namespaces

Now that you know how to create a UTS namespace, this section demonstrates how to add more namespaces.

First, we add more clone flags, in order to create more namespaces for the container we are creating:

```go
package main
import (
  "fmt"
  "os"
  "os/exec"
  "syscall"
)
func main() {
  cmd := exec.Command("/bin/bash")
  cmd.Stdin = os.Stdin
  cmd.Stdout = os.Stdout
  cmd.Stderr = os.Stderr
  cmd.Env = []string{"name=shashank"}
  //command below creates the UTS, PID and IPC , NETWORK and
  USERNAMESPACES
  cmd.SysProcAttr = &syscall.SysProcAttr{
      Cloneflags: syscall.CLONE_NEWNS |
          syscall.CLONE_NEWUTS |
          syscall.CLONE_NEWIPC |
          syscall.CLONE_NEWPID |
          syscall.CLONE_NEWNET |
          syscall.CLONE_NEWUSER,
  }
  if err := cmd.Run(); err != nil {
   fmt.Printf("Error running the /bin/bash command -
   %s\n", err)
   os.Exit(1)
  }
}
```

In the code above we added more namespaces via the clone flag. We build and run the program as follows:

```
root@osboxes:~/book_prep# ./myuts
nobody@osboxes:/root/book_prep$ ls -li /proc/self/ns/ total 0
17488 lrwxrwxrwx 1 nobody nogroup 0 Jul 14 16:10 cgroup ->
'cgroup:[4026531835]'
17483 lrwxrwxrwx 1 nobody nogroup 0 Jul 14 16:10 ipc ->
'ipc:[4026532335]'
17487 lrwxrwxrwx 1 nobody nogroup 0 Jul 14 16:10 mnt ->
'mnt:[4026532333]'
17481 lrwxrwxrwx 1 nobody nogroup 0 Jul 14 16:10 net ->
'net:[4026532338]'
17484 lrwxrwxrwx 1 nobody nogroup 0 Jul 14 16:10 pid ->
'pid:[4026532336]'
17485 lrwxrwxrwx 1 nobody nogroup 0 Jul 14 16:10 pid_for_
children -> 'pid:[4026532336]'
17489 lrwxrwxrwx 1 nobody nogroup 0 Jul 14 16:10 time ->
'time:[4026531834]'
17490 lrwxrwxrwx 1 nobody nogroup 0 Jul 14 16:10 time_for_
children -> 'time:[4026531834]'
17486 lrwxrwxrwx 1 nobody nogroup 0 Jul 14 16:10 user ->
'user:[4026532325]'
17482 lrwxrwxrwx 1 nobody nogroup 0 Jul 14 16:10 uts ->
'uts:[4026532334]'
```

We have the namespaces this container belongs to. Now we see that the ownership belongs to nobody. This is because we also used a user namespace as a clone flag. The container is now within a new user namespace. User namespaces require that we map the user from the namespace to the host. Since we have not done anything yet, we still see nobody as the user.

We now add user mapping to the code:

```go
package main

import (
    "fmt"
    "os"
    "os/exec"
    "syscall"
)

func main() {
    cmd := exec.Command("/bin/bash")
    cmd.Stdin = os.Stdin
    cmd.Stdout = os.Stdout
    cmd.Stderr = os.Stderr
    cmd.Env = []string{"name=shashank"}

    cmd.SysProcAttr = &syscall.SysProcAttr{
        Cloneflags: syscall.CLONE_NEWNS |
            syscall.CLONE_NEWUTS |
            syscall.CLONE_NEWIPC |
            syscall.CLONE_NEWPID |
            syscall.CLONE_NEWNET |
            syscall.CLONE_NEWUSER,
        UidMappings: []syscall.SysProcIDMap{
            {
                ContainerID: 0,
                HostID:      os.Getuid(),
                Size:        1,
            },
        },
```

```
    GidMappings: []syscall.SysProcIDMap{
        {
            ContainerID: 0,
            HostID:      os.Getgid(),
            Size:        1,
        },
    },
}

if err := cmd.Run(); err != nil {
    fmt.Printf("Error running the /bin/bash command -
    %s\n", err)
    os.Exit(1)
}
}
```

You can see that we have UidMappings and GidMappings. We have a
field called ContainerID, which we are setting to 0. This means we are
mapping the uid and gid 0 within the container to the uid and gid of the
user who launched the process.

There is one interesting aspect I would like to touch upon in the
context of user namespaces: you don't need to be the root on the host
in order to create a user namespace. This provides a way to create
namespaces, and thereby containers, without being the root on the
machine, which is a big security win, as providing root access to a process
can be hazardous. If programs are launched as the root, any compromise
to those programs can give root privileges to the attacker. In turn, the
whole machine gets compromised.

Technically, you can be non-root on the host and then create a user
namespace and other namespaces within that user namespace. Mind you,
all the other namespaces, if launched without a user namespace, will need
root access.

If we take the previous example, where we are passing all the flags together, the system first creates a user namespace and places all the other namespaces within that user namespace.

I cannot cover the user namespace topic in its entirety here, but it is an interesting area for curious readers to explore. One area I can mention straightaway is that of Docker builds, wherein we need root access to build an image within a container. This is necessary for many reasons, as we need some layered file systems mounted within the container, and creating a new mount requires root privilege.

The same holds for setting up virtual network devices like virtual ethernet (veth) pair in order to wire containers to the host. Having said that, there has been momentum in the area of *rootless* containers, which allow developers to run containers without the root. If you want to read about this topic in more detail, check out the following: `https://rootlesscontaine.rs/` and `https://github.com/rootless-containers`.

What we have achieved thus far is the ability to launch a process within a set of namespaces. But we definitely need more, including a way to initialize these namespaces before we launch the container.

Back to the program we created. Let's build and run it:

```
root@osboxes:~/book_prep# ./myuts
root@osboxes:/root/book_prep# whoami
root
root@osboxes:/root/book_prep# id
uid=0(root) gid=0(root) groups=0(root)
```

Now we see that the user within the container is the root.

The program checks the first argument. If the first command is run, then the program executes /proc/self/exe, which is simply saying "execute yourself" (/proc/self/exe is the copy of the binary image of the caller itself).

You might be wondering why we need to execute `/proc/self/exe`. When we execute this command, it launches the same binary with some arguments (in our case, we pass `fork` as the argument to it). Once we are into different namespaces, we need some setup for the namespaces, like setting the hostname, before we launch the process within the container.

Executing `/proc/self/exe` gives us the opportunity to set up the namespaces like so:

1. Set the hostname.

2. Within the mount namespace, we do a pivot root, which allows us to switch the root file system. It does this by copying the old root to some other directory and making the new path the new root. This pivot root has to be done from within the mount namespace, as we don't want to move the `rootfs` off the host. We also mount the `proc` file system. This is done because the mount namespace inherits the `proc` of the host and we want a `proc` mount within the mount namespace.

3. Once the namespaces are initialized and set up, we invoke the container process (in this case, the shell).

Running this program launches the shell into a sandbox confined by the `proc` mount, and `uts` namespace.

Now we work on initializing the namespaces before launching the process within the container. In the following example, we will have a different hostname in the `uts` namespace. In the following code, we make the required changes.

We have a function parent that performs the following:

1. Clones the namespaces.

2. Launches the same process again via `/proc/self/exe` and passes a child as the parameter.

Now the process is called again. Checks in the main function lead to invocations of the child function. Now you can see that we cloned the namespaces. All we do now is change the hostname to myhost within the uts namespace. Once that is done, we invoke the binary passed as the command-line parameter (in this case, /bin/bash).

Launching a Shell Program Within the Container

The previous sections explained how to create different Linux namespaces. This section explains how to enter those namespaces. Entering the confines of the namespaces can be done by launching a program/process within the namespaces. The following program launches a shell program within these namespaces.

```
package main
import (
    "fmt"
    "os"
    "os/exec"
    "syscall"
)
func main() {
switch os.Args[1] {
    case "parent":
        parent()
    case "child":
        child()
    default:
        panic("help")
    }
}
```

```go
// the parent function invoked from the main program which sets
up the needed namespaces
func parent() {
    cmd := exec.Command("/proc/self/exe",
append([]string{"child"}, os.Args[2:]...)...)
    cmd.Stdin = os.Stdin
    cmd.Stdout = os.Stdout
    cmd.Stderr = os.Stderr
    cmd.Env = []string{"name=shashank"}
    cmd.SysProcAttr = &syscall.SysProcAttr{
        Cloneflags: syscall.CLONE_NEWNS |
            syscall.CLONE_NEWUTS |
            syscall.CLONE_NEWIPC |
            syscall.CLONE_NEWPID |
            syscall.CLONE_NEWNET |
            syscall.CLONE_NEWUSER,
    UidMappings: []syscall.SysProcIDMap{
            {
                ContainerID: 0,
                HostID: os.Getuid(),
                Size: 1,
            },
        },
        GidMappings: []syscall.SysProcIDMap{
            {
                ContainerID: 0,
                HostID: os.Getgid(),
                Size: 1,
            },
        },
    }
```

```go
    must(cmd.Run())
}
// this is the child process which is a copy of the parent
program itself.
func child () {
cmd := exec.Command(os.Args[2], os.Args[3:]...)
    cmd.Stdin = os.Stdin
    cmd.Stdout = os.Stdout
    cmd.Stderr = os.Stderr
//the command below sets the hostname to myhost. Idea here is
to showcase the use of UTS namespace
must(syscall.Sethostname([]byte("myhost")))
// this command executes the shell which is passed as a program
argument
must(cmd.Run())
}
func must(err error) {
    if err != nil {
        fmt.Printf("Error - %s\n", err)
    }
}
```

Upon executing the program, we can launch the binary within the new namespaces (note that the hostname is set to myhost):

```
root@osboxes:~/book_prep# ./myuts parent /bin/bash
root@myhost:/root/book_prep# hostname
myhost
root@myhost:/root/book_prep#
```

After the uts namespace, it's time to get more adventurous. We now work on initializing the mount namespace.

One thing to understand here is that all mounts from the host are inherited within the mount namespace. Therefore, we need a mechanism to clear the mounts and only make mounts for the mount namespace visible within that namespace.

Before we move ahead, one of the things to understand conceptually is the system call `pivot_root`. This system call allows us to change the root file system for the process. It mounts the old root to some other directory (in the following example, the author used `pivot_root` as the directory to mount the old root on) and mounts the new directory on /. This allows us to clear all the host mounts within the namespace.

Again, we need to be inside the mount namespace before we invoke the `pivot_root`. Since we already have a hook on namespace initialization (via the `/proc/self/exe` hack), we need to introduce a pivot root mechanism.

Providing the Root File System

We will use the `rootfs` from busybox (`rootfs` tar file), which you can download from

```
https://github.com/ericchiang/containers-from-scratch/
releases/download/v0.1.0/rootfs.tar.gz
```

After downloading `rootfs.tar.gz`, extract it to `/root/book_prep/rootfs` in your system. This location is referred to in this code as the location of `rootfs`. As shown in Figure 6-1, the contents of `/root/book_prep/rootfs` should look the same on your system.

```
root@osboxes:~/book_prep/rootfs# ls -l
total 48
drwxr-xr-x 2 root root 12288 Jun 23  2016 bin
drwxr-xr-x 2 sys  sys   4096 Jun 23  2016 dev
drwxr-xr-x 2 root root  4096 Jun 23  2016 etc
drwxr-xr-x 2   99   99  4096 Jun 23  2016 home
drwxr-xr-x 2 root root  4096 Jun 23  2016 lib
lrwxrwxrwx 1 root root     3 Jun 23  2016 lib64 -> lib
drwxr-xr-x 2 root root  4096 Jul 11 07:55 proc
drwxr-xr-x 2 root root  4096 Jun 23  2016 root
drwxrwxrwt 2 root root  4096 Jun 23  2016 tmp
drwxr-xr-x 3 root root  4096 Jun 23  2016 usr
drwxr-xr-x 4 root root  4096 Jun 23  2016 var
root@osboxes:~/book_prep/rootfs#
```

Figure 6-1. *The contents of the* /root/book_prep/rootfs *path*

After extracting the rootfs, we can see the directory structure under the rootfs directory:

```
root@osboxes:~/book_prep/rootfs# ls
bin  dev  etc  home  lib  lib64  root  tmp  usr  var
root@osboxes:~/book_prep/rootfs# cd ..
root@osboxes:~/book_prep# 
```

The following program does a pivot root to the rootfs within the mount namespace.

The mount namespace becomes important, as it allows us to sandbox the file system mounts. This is one way to get an isolated view of the file system hierarchy and see what is present on the host or on different sandboxes running on the same host.

As an example, assume there are two sandboxes—sandboxA and sandboxB—running on the host. When sandboxA gets its own mounts, its file system sees a different and isolated mount from what sandboxB sees, and neither can see the mounts of the host. This provides security at the file system level, as individual sandboxes cannot access files from different sandboxes or from the host.

```go
package main

import (
    "fmt"
    "os"
    "os/exec"
    "path/filepath"
    "syscall"
)

func pivotRoot(newroot string) error {
    putold := filepath.Join(newroot, "/.pivot_root")
    //if err != nil {
        //return err
//    }
    // Ensure putold is removed after the function returns

    // Bind mount newroot to putold to make putold a valid
    mount point
    if err := syscall.Mount(newroot, newroot, "", syscall.MS_
    BIND|syscall.MS_REC, ""); err != nil {
    return err
}

// create putold directory
if err := os.MkdirAll(putold, 0700); err != nil{
 return err
}
    // Call pivot_root
    if err := syscall.PivotRoot(newroot, putold); err != nil {
        return err
    }

    // Change the current working directory to the new root
```

```go
    if err := os.Chdir("/"); err != nil {
        return err
    }

    // Unmount putold, which now lives at /.pivot_root
    if err := syscall.Unmount("/.pivot_root", syscall.MNT_
    DETACH); err != nil {
        return err
    }

    return nil
}

func parent() {
    cmd := exec.Command("/proc/self/exe",
    append([]string{"child"}, os.Args[2:]...)...)
    cmd.Stdin = os.Stdin
    cmd.Stdout = os.Stdout
    cmd.Stderr = os.Stderr
    cmd.Env = []string{"name=shashank"}
    cmd.SysProcAttr = &syscall.SysProcAttr{
        Cloneflags: syscall.CLONE_NEWNS |
            syscall.CLONE_NEWUTS |
            syscall.CLONE_NEWIPC |
            syscall.CLONE_NEWPID |
            syscall.CLONE_NEWNET |
            syscall.CLONE_NEWUSER,
        UidMappings: []syscall.SysProcIDMap{
            {
                ContainerID: 0,
                HostID:      os.Getuid(),
                Size:        1,
            },
        },
```

```go
        GidMappings: []syscall.SysProcIDMap{
            {
                ContainerID: 0,
                HostID:      os.Getgid(),
                Size:        1,
            },
        },
    }

    must(cmd.Run())
}

func child() {
    // Set the hostname for the child process
    must(syscall.Sethostname([]byte("myhost")))

    // Now execute the command specified in the command-line
    arguments
    cmd := exec.Command(os.Args[2], os.Args[3:]...)
    cmd.Stdin = os.Stdin
    cmd.Stdout = os.Stdout
    cmd.Stderr = os.Stderr
    must(mountProc("/root/book_prep/rootfs"))
    must(syscall.Sethostname([]byte("myhost")))
if err := pivotRoot("/root/book_prep/rootfs"); err != nil{
fmt.Printf("Error running pivot_root - %s\n",err)
os.Exit(1)
}
    must(cmd.Run())
}

func must(err error) {
```

```go
    if err != nil {
        fmt.Printf("Error - %s\n", err)
    }
}

func main() {
    switch os.Args[1] {
    case "parent":
        parent()
    case "child":
        child()
    default:
        panic("help")
    }
}
// this function mounts the proc filesystem within the
// new mount namespace
func mountProc(newroot string) error {
    source := "proc"
    target := filepath.Join(newroot, "/proc")
    fstype := "proc"
    flags := 0
    data := ""
//make a Mount system call to mount the proc filesystem within
the mount namespace
    os.MkdirAll(target, 0755)
    if err := syscall.Mount(
        source,
        target,
        fstype,
        uintptr(flags),
        data,
```

```
); err != nil {
    return err
}
return nil
}
```

After executing the following program, we can see the directories under rootfs, see that the hostname has changed, and see the uid as 0 (the root within the container):

```
root@osboxes:~/book_prep# ./myuts parent /bin/sh
/ # ls
bin    dev    etc    home    lib    lib64    root    tmp    usr    var
/ # hostname
myhost
/ # id
uid=0(root) gid=0(root) groups=0(root)
/ # |
```

We still have a problem. By default, the proc mount is not there. We need the proc mount to provide information about different processes running within the namespace and as an interface to the kernel for other utilities, as explained in the pseudo file systems in Chapter 5. We need to mount the proc file system within the mount namespace.

The Mount Proc File System

Next we add the new mountProc function to the program:

```
func mountProc(newroot string) error {
    source := "proc"
    target := filepath.Join(newroot, "/proc")
    fstype := "proc"
    flags := 0
    data := ""
```

```
//make a Mount system call to mount the proc filesystem within
the mount namespace
    os.MkdirAll(target, 0755)
    if err := syscall.Mount(
        source,
        target,
        fstype,
        uintptr(flags),
        data,
    ); err != nil {
        return err
    }
    return nil
}
```

Now, when we run ps inside the container to list the processes running within the sandbox, we get the output shown here. The reason for this is that ps uses the /proc file system.

```
root@osboxes:~/book_prep# ./myuts parent /bin/sh
/ # ps
PID   USER      TIME   COMMAND
    1 root      0:00 /proc/self/exe child /bin/sh
    6 root      0:00 /bin/sh
    7 root      0:00 ps
/ # |
```

We can use the nsenter command to enter the created container namespaces. To try that, let the created container be in the running state and open another Linux terminal. Then run this command:

ps -ef | grep /bin/sh

You should see output similar to the following. In my case, my container's PID is 5387. Users should use the PIDs on their own machines.

```
root@osboxes:~# ps -ef | grep /bin/sh
root       5387   3829  0 14:00 pts/1    00:00:00 ./myuts parent /bin/sh
root       5392   5387  0 14:00 pts/1    00:00:00 /proc/self/exe child /bin/sh
root       5397   5392  0 14:00 pts/1    00:00:00 /bin/sh
root       5574   5560  0 14:04 pts/0    00:00:00 grep --color=auto /bin/sh
root@osboxes:~# nsenter -a -t 5397 /bin/bash
nsenter: failed to execute /bin/bash: No such file or directory
root@osboxes:~# nsenter -a -t 5397 /bin/sh
/ # |
```

Executing `nsenter -a -t 5387 /bin/sh` allows this shell to be created in the namespaces of the process with the PID 5387, as shown.

Overall the code is doing the following things:

- The program accepts a command-line argument to determine whether it will act as the parent or the child process.

- If it's the "parent" process, it creates a child process with certain configurations.

- The child process is created with isolated namespaces for the mount, UTS (host and domain name), IPC (inter-process communication), PID (process ID), network, and user.

- The `pivotRoot()` function is used to change the root file system. It sets up a temporary directory and performs the root file system change operation.

- The "parent" process starts the child process and waits for it to finish executing.

- If it's the "child" process, it executes a command based on the provided arguments.

- The `mountProc()` function is used to mount the /proc file system within the new namespace.

- The hostname is set to a specific value.

- The pivotRoot() function is called to change the root file system to a different directory.

- The specified command is executed within the new environment.

- There's also a utility function called must() that handles error checking and printing error messages.

Enabling the Network for the Container

In previous sections, we created a container with uts, PID, and mount namespaces. We didn't add the network namespace. In this section, we discuss how to set up network namespaces for the container.

Before we delve into the networking topic, I will provide a brief primer on virtual devices in Linux, which are essential for understanding container-based networks, or for that matter any virtual networking.

Virtual Networking: A Brief Primer

In a virtualized world, there is a need to send packets across virtual machines to the actual physical devices, between VMs, or between different containers. We need a mechanism to use virtualized devices in this way. Linux provides a mechanism to create virtual network devices, called tun and tap. The tun device acts at Layer 3 of the network stack, which means it receives the IP packets. The tap device acts at Layer 2, where it receives raw Ethernet packets.

Now one might ask, what are these devices used for? Consider a scenario where containerA needs to send packets outbound to another container. The packets from one packet are transmitted to the host machine, which smartly uses a tap device to pass the packet to a software bridge. The bridge can then be connected to another container.

Let's see how these tap devices work with a simple example. The
following creates two tap devices, called mytap1 and mytap2:

```
jain_sm@instance-1:~$ sudo su
root@instance-1:/home/jain_sm# ip tuntap add name mytap1 mode tap
root@instance-1:/home/jain_sm# ip tuntap add name mytap2 mode tap
```

Listing the tap devices, we can see there are two network interfaces:

```
root@instance-1:/home/jain_sm# ip addr show
1: lo: <LOOPBACK,UP,LOWER_UP> mtu 65536 qdisc noqueue state UNKNOWN group default qlen 1000
    link/loopback 00:00:00:00:00:00 brd 00:00:00:00:00:00
    inet 127.0.0.1/8 scope host lo
       valid_lft forever preferred_lft forever
    inet6 ::1/128 scope host
       valid_lft forever preferred_lft forever
2: ens4: <BROADCAST,MULTICAST,UP,LOWER_UP> mtu 1460 qdisc mq state UP group default qlen 1000
    link/ether 42:01:0a:80:00:02 brd ff:ff:ff:ff:ff:ff
    inet 10.128.0.2/32 brd 10.128.0.2 scope global ens4
       valid_lft forever preferred_lft forever
    inet6 fe80::4001:aff:fe80:2/64 scope link
       valid_lft forever preferred_lft forever
3: mytap1: <BROADCAST,MULTICAST> mtu 1500 qdisc noop state DOWN group default qlen 1000
    link/ether 1e:34:fc:78:28:f6 brd ff:ff:ff:ff:ff:ff
    inet 10.0.0.10/32 scope global mytap1
       valid_lft forever preferred_lft forever
4: mytap2: <BROADCAST,MULTICAST> mtu 1500 qdisc noop state DOWN group default qlen 1000
    link/ether 36:df:e9:2c:ad:76 brd ff:ff:ff:ff:ff:ff
    inet 10.0.0.11/32 scope global mytap2
       valid_lft forever preferred_lft forever
```

We assign IP addresses to these devices:

```
root@instance-1:/home/jain_sm# ip addr add 10.0.0.10 dev mytap1
root@instance-1:/home/jain_sm# ip addr add 10.0.0.11 dev mytap2
```

Running a simple ping from one device to the other results in the
following:

```
root@instance-1:/home/jain_sm# ping -I 10.0.0.10 -c1 10.0.0.11
PING 10.0.0.11 (10.0.0.11) from 10.0.0.10 : 56(84) bytes of data.
64 bytes from 10.0.0.11: icmp_seq=1 ttl=64 time=0.054 ms

--- 10.0.0.11 ping statistics ---
1 packets transmitted, 1 received, 0% packet loss, time 0ms
rtt min/avg/max/mdev = 0.054/0.054/0.054/0.000 ms
```

In these examples, we explicitly created two tap devices and tried a ping between the two.

We can also use veth pairs, which can be thought of as virtual cables that connect the virtual devices. They are used in openstack to connect software bridges.

First, we create a veth pair as follows:

```
root@instance-1:/home/jain_sm# ip link add firsttap type veth peer name secondtap
```

This creates two tap interfaces, called firstap and secondtap.

Now, we add IP addresses to the tap devices and run a ping:

```
root@instance-1:/home/jain_sm# ip addr add 10.0.0.12 dev firsttap
root@instance-1:/home/jain_sm# ip addr add 10.0.0.13 dev secondtap
root@instance-1:/home/jain_sm# ping -I 10.0.0.12 -c1 10.0.0.13
PING 10.0.0.13 (10.0.0.13) from 10.0.0.12 : 56(84) bytes of data.
64 bytes from 10.0.0.13: icmp_seq=1 ttl=64 time=0.032 ms
```

With a basic understanding of tun and tap devices, let's move on to how the networking setup should work between the namespace created for the container and the host's namespace. For that process, we follow these steps:

1. Create a Linux bridge on the host.

2. Create a veth pair.

3. Connect one end of the veth pair must be connected to the bridge.

4. Connect the other end of the bridge to the network interface on the container namespace.

These steps are illustrated in Figure 6-2.

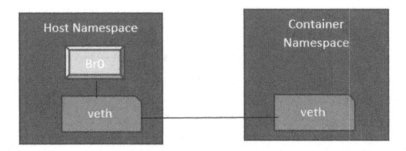

Figure 6-2. *Networking between the container's namespace and the host's namespace*

Now we modify the code to enable the network namespace:

```
package main

import (
    "fmt"
    "os"
    "os/exec"
    "time"
    "path/filepath"
    "syscall"
    "net"
)

func pivotRoot(newroot string) error {
    putold := filepath.Join(newroot, "/.pivot_root")
    //if err != nil {
        //return err
//    }
    // Ensure putold is removed after the function returns

    // Bind mount newroot to putold to make putold a valid
    mount point
```

```go
    if err := syscall.Mount(newroot, newroot, "", syscall.MS_
    BIND|syscall.MS_REC, ""); err != nil {
    return err
}

// create putold directory
if err := os.MkdirAll(putold, 0700); err != nil{
 return err
}
    // Call pivot_root
    if err := syscall.PivotRoot(newroot, putold); err != nil {
        return err
    }

    // Change the current working directory to the new root
    if err := os.Chdir("/"); err != nil {
        return err
    }

    // Unmount putold, which now lives at /.pivot_root
    if err := syscall.Unmount("/.pivot_root", syscall.MNT_
    DETACH); err != nil {
        return err
    }

    return nil
}

func parent() {
    cmd := exec.Command("/proc/self/exe",
    append([]string{"child"}, os.Args[2:]...)...)
    cmd.Stdin = os.Stdin
    cmd.Stdout = os.Stdout
    cmd.Stderr = os.Stderr
```

```go
    cmd.Env = []string{"name=shashank"}
    cmd.SysProcAttr = &syscall.SysProcAttr{
        Cloneflags: syscall.CLONE_NEWNS |
            syscall.CLONE_NEWUTS |
            syscall.CLONE_NEWIPC |
            syscall.CLONE_NEWPID |
            syscall.CLONE_NEWNET |
            syscall.CLONE_NEWUSER,
        UidMappings: []syscall.SysProcIDMap{
            {
                ContainerID: 0,
                HostID:      os.Getuid(),
                Size:        1,
            },
        },
        GidMappings: []syscall.SysProcIDMap{
            {
                ContainerID: 0,
                HostID:      os.Getgid(),
                Size:        1,
            },
        },
    }

            must(cmd.Start())

    pid := fmt.Sprintf("%d", cmd.Process.Pid)
    fmt.Printf("obtaibed pid %s",pid)
// Code below does the following
// Creates the bridge on the host
// Creates the veth pair
// Attaches one end of veth to bridge
```

```go
// Attaches the other end to the network namespace. This is
interesting
// as we now have access to the host side and the network side
until // we block.
netsetgoCmd := exec.Command("/usr/local/bin/netsetgo",
"-pid", pid)
  if err := netsetgoCmd.Run(); err != nil {
    fmt.Printf("Error running netsetgo - %s\n", err)
    os.Exit(1)
  }
  if err := cmd.Wait(); err != nil {
    fmt.Printf("Error waiting for reexec.Command - %s\n", err)
    os.Exit(1)
  }

}

func child() {
    // Set the hostname for the child process
    must(syscall.Sethostname([]byte("myhost")))

    // Now execute the command specified in the command-line
    arguments
    cmd := exec.Command(os.Args[2], os.Args[3:]...)
    cmd.Stdin = os.Stdin
    cmd.Stdout = os.Stdout
    cmd.Stderr = os.Stderr
    must(mountProc("/root/book_prep/rootfs"))
    must(syscall.Sethostname([]byte("myhost")))
if err := pivotRoot("/root/book_prep/rootfs"); err != nil{
fmt.Printf("Error running pivot_root - %s\n",err)
os.Exit(1)
}
```

```go
if err := waitForNetwork(); err != nil {
                fmt.Printf("Error waiting for network -
                %s\n", err)
                os.Exit(1)
        }

    must(cmd.Run())
}

func must(err error) {
    if err != nil {
        fmt.Printf("Error - %s\n", err)
    }
}

func main() {
    switch os.Args[1] {
    case "parent":
        parent()
    case "child":
        child()
    default:
        panic("help")
    }
}

func waitForNetwork() error {
  maxWait := time.Second * 3
    checkInterval := time.Second
    timeStarted := time.Now()
    for {
        interfaces, err := net.Interfaces()
        if err != nil {
```

```go
        return err
      }
      // pretty basic check ...
      // > 1 as a lo device will already exist
      if len(interfaces) > 1 {
        return nil
      }
      if time.Since(timeStarted) > maxWait {
      return fmt.Errorf("Timeout after %s waiting for network",
      maxWait)
      }
      time.Sleep(checkInterval)
      }
}

// this function mounts the proc filesystem within the
// new mount namespace
func mountProc(newroot string) error {
    source := "proc"
    target := filepath.Join(newroot, "/proc")
    fstype := "proc"
    flags := 0
    data := ""
//make a Mount system call to mount the proc filesystem within
the mount namespace
    os.MkdirAll(target, 0755)
    if err := syscall.Mount(
        source,
        target,
        fstype,
        uintptr(flags),
        data,
```

```
); err != nil {
    return err
}
return nil
}
```

There are a few aspects that are worth considering here. In the earlier code examples, we initialized namespaces (like changing the hostname and pivot root) in the child method. Then we launched the shell (/bin/sh) within the namespaces. This mechanism worked because we just needed to initialize the namespaces, and that was being done within the namespaces themselves. When it comes to the network namespace, we need to carry out certain activities like the following:

- Create a bridge on the host.

- Create the veth pair and make one end connect to the bridge on the host and the other end within the network namespace.

The problem with the current way is that when we launch the shell, we remain in the namespace until we purposely exit it. So, we need a way to return the code immediately in the API so we can execute the network setup on the host and join the veth pairs.

Fortunately, the cmd.Run command can be broken into two parts:

- cmd.Start() returns immediately.

- cmd.Wait() blocks until the shell is exited.

We use this to our advantage in the parent() function method. We execute the cmd.Start() funciton, which returns immediately.

After the start method, we use a library called netsetgo (created by Ed King from Pivotal). It does the following.

1. Creates the bridge on the host.

2. Creates the veth pair.

3. Attaches one end of the veth pair to the bridge.

4. Attaches the other end to the network namespace.
    This is interesting, as we now have access to the host
    side and the network side until we block.

Follow the instructions to download and install netsetgo:

```
wget "https://github.com/teddyking/netsetgo/releases/
download/0.0.1/netsetgo"
sudo mv netsetgo /usr/local/bin/
sudo chown root:root /usr/local/bin/netsetgo
sudo chmod 4755 /usr/local/bin/netsetgo
```

In fact, a lot of these explanations are adapted from Ed King's
examples.

The related code snippet is shown here:

```
must(cmd.Start())
pid := fmt.Sprintf("%d", cmd.Process.Pid)
netsetgoCmd := exec.Command("/usr/local/bin/netsetgo",
"-pid", pid)
if err := netsetgoCmd.Run(); err != nil {
   fmt.Printf("Error running netsetgo - %s\n", err)
   os.Exit(1)
}
if err := cmd.Wait(); err != nil {
   fmt.Printf("Error waiting for reexec.Command - %s\n", err)
   os.Exit(1)
}
```

Once this is done, we use cmd.Wait(), which relaunches the program (/proc/self/exe). Then we execute the child process and go ahead with all the other initializations. After the initializations, we can launch the shell within the namespaces.

Next, we should verify the network communication from the host to the container and from the container to the host. First run this program:

```
/myuts parent /bin/sh
```

Within the container shell, run the ip a command. You should see the container's IP address, as shown here:

```
# ip a
1: lo: <LOOPBACK> mtu 65536 qdisc noop state DOWN group default
qlen 1000
    link/loopback 00:00:00:00:00:00 brd 00:00:00:00:00:00
5: veth1@if6: <BROADCAST,MULTICAST,UP,LOWER_UP> mtu 1500 qdisc
noqueue state UP group default qlen 1000
    link/ether e2:8c:f0:b8:35:45 brd ff:ff:ff:ff:ff:ff
    inet 10.10.10.2/24 scope global veth1
       valid_lft forever preferred_lft forever
    inet6 fe80::e08c:f0ff:feb8:3545/64 scope link
       valid_lft forever preferred_lft forever
```

Keep the container running and open another terminal (a bash shell) on the host. Run the following command, which pings the container's IP:

```
ping 10.10.10.2
```

```
osboxes@osboxes: ~
osboxes@osboxes:~$ ping 10.10.10.2
PING 10.10.10.2 (10.10.10.2) 56(84) bytes of data.
64 bytes from 10.10.10.2: icmp_seq=1 ttl=64 time=0.098 ms
64 bytes from 10.10.10.2: icmp_seq=2 ttl=64 time=0.045 ms
^C
--- 10.10.10.2 ping statistics ---
2 packets transmitted, 2 received, 0% packet loss, time 24ms
rtt min/avg/max/mdev = 0.045/0.071/0.098/0.027 ms
osboxes@osboxes:~$
```

Note that we are able to ping the container's IP address from the host.

Now try pinging the host IP address from the container. First, get the host IP address by running the ifconfig command. As you can see here, my host IP address is 10.0.2.15:

```
osboxes@osboxes: ~
osboxes@osboxes:~$ ifconfig
org0: flags=4163<UP,BROADCAST,RUNNING,MULTICAST>  mtu 1500
        inet 10.10.10.1  netmask 255.255.255.0  broadcast 0.0.0.0
        inet6 fe80::ec28:c2ff:fe14:dc29  prefixlen 64  scopeid 0x20<link>
        ether 4a:d8:23:9f:4a:2e  txqueuelen 0  (Ethernet)
        RX packets 45  bytes 2864 (2.8 KB)
        RX errors 0  dropped 0  overruns 0  frame 0
        TX packets 369  bytes 20423 (20.4 KB)
        TX errors 0  dropped 0 overruns 0  carrier 0  collisions 0

enp0s3: flags=4163<UP,BROADCAST,RUNNING,MULTICAST>  mtu 1500
        inet 10.0.2.15  netmask 255.255.255.0  broadcast 10.0.2.255
        inet6 fe80::ce61:ba4f:3cb9:32c0  prefixlen 64  scopeid 0x20<link>
        ether 08:00:27:92:f8:21  txqueuelen 1000  (Ethernet)
        RX packets 611  bytes 510075 (510.0 KB)
        RX errors 0  dropped 0  overruns 0  frame 0
        TX packets 398  bytes 44160 (44.1 KB)
        TX errors 0  dropped 0 overruns 0  carrier 0  collisions 0
```

Now ping this host IP address from the container:

```
/ # ping 10.0.2.15
PING 10.0.2.15 (10.0.2.15): 56 data bytes
64 bytes from 10.0.2.15: seq=0 ttl=64 time=0.050 ms
64 bytes from 10.0.2.15: seq=1 ttl=64 time=0.061 ms
64 bytes from 10.0.2.15: seq=2 ttl=64 time=0.078 ms
64 bytes from 10.0.2.15: seq=3 ttl=64 time=0.083 ms
^C
--- 10.0.2.15 ping statistics ---
4 packets transmitted, 4 packets received, 0% packet loss
round-trip min/avg/max = 0.050/0.068/0.083 ms
/ #
```

131

As you can see, we could ping from the container to the host as well as from the host to the container, so networking communication is working both ways.

Overall the code does the following things:

- The program accepts a command-line argument to determine whether it will act as the "parent" or "child" process.

- If it's the "parent" process, it executes the parent() function. If it's the "child" process, it executes the child() function. If neither "parent" nor "child" is provided as an argument, the program raises a panic with the message help.

- The waitForNetwork() function is defined to check for network availability. It repeatedly checks the network interfaces until either a network interface other than the loopback interface is found or a timeout of 3 seconds is reached.

- The mountProc() function is defined to mount the /proc file system within a specified root directory. It creates the target directory if it doesn't exist and mounts the /proc file system onto that directory.

- The pivotRoot() function is defined to pivot the root file system. It sets up a temporary directory (putold) to satisfy the pivot_root requirement that the new root and putold directories must reside on different file systems. It mounts the new root directory onto itself, creates the putold directory, performs the pivot operation to change the root file system, sets the current working directory to the new root, unmounts putold, and removes it.

- The parent() function is defined to create a child process with isolated namespaces. It uses the exec. Command function to execute a command within a child process. The command is the current program itself, with additional arguments to indicate it should act as the "child" process. It sets the standard input, output, and error streams for the child process, sets an environment variable, and configures various namespaces (CLONE_NEWNS, CLONE_NEWUTS, CLONE_NEWIPC, CLONE_NEWPID, CLONE_ NEWNET, and CLONE_NEWUSER). It also maps the user and group IDs from the host to the container namespaces. The child process is started, and its PID is obtained.

- The netsetgoCmd command is executed to set up network-related configurations for the child process. It creates a bridge, a virtual Ethernet pair, and attaches one end of the virtual Ethernet to the bridge and the other end to the child process's network namespace.

- The child() function is defined to execute a command within a child process. It uses exec.Command to execute the command specified in the program's command-line arguments. It sets the standard input, output, and error streams for the child process. It calls mountProc() to mount the /proc file system, sets the hostname, calls pivotRoot() to change the root file system, waits for the network to be available using waitForNetwork(), and starts the command execution.

- The must() function is a utility function used to handle errors. If an error is passed to it, it prints an error message.

Let's recap what we have achieved thus far:

- We created a container with unshare and demonstrated the ability to change the hostname within a uts namespace.

- We created a container with Golang with namespaces like UTS and user.

- We added a mount namespaces and demonstrated how a separate proc file system can be mounted within the namespace.

- We added network capabilities to the namespace, which allow us to communicate between the container namespaces and the host namespace.

Enabling Cgroups for the Container

We earlier mounted a cgroup on /root/mygrp. We created a directory child within it. Now we will put our process within the cgroup and cap its maximum memory.

Here is the sample code snippet:

```go
func enableCgroup() {
  cgroups := "/root/mygrp"
  pids := filepath.Join(cgroups, "child")
  must(ioutil.WriteFile(filepath.Join(pids, "memory.max"),
  []byte("2M"), 0700))
  must(ioutil.WriteFile(filepath.Join(pids, "cgroup.procs"),
  []byte(strconv.Itoa(os.Getpid())), 0700))
}
```

In this code snippet, we add the PID of the process we create within the container (/bin/sh) to the `cgroup.procs` file and cap the maximum memory for the process to 2MB.

Before executing this code, you need to make one configuration change to the OS. Open the /etc/default/grub file using Nano or your favorite editor:

nano /etc/default/grub

In this file, you have to modify the GRUB_CMDLINE_LINUX_DEFAULT key to add systemd.unified_cgroup_hierarchy=1. Refer to the following image for clarification.

GRUB_CMDLINE_LINUX_DEFAULT="quiet splash systemd.unified_cgroup_hierarchy=1"

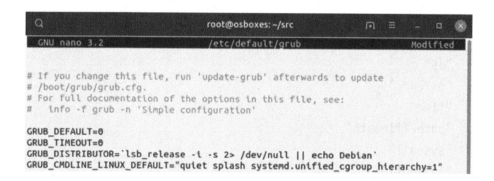

After the update, run the command and reboot the system:

sudo update-grub

After the system reboots, run this command:

cat /proc/cmdline

```
root@osboxes:~/src# cat /proc/cmdline
BOOT_IMAGE=/vmlinuz-5.0.0-13-generic root=UUID=03e8c4b4-3806-4e6c-a727-f36ad802f
f1d ro quiet splash systemd.unified_cgroup_hierarchy=1
root@osboxes:~/src#
```

You should see systemd.unified_cgroup_hierarchy=1 as the BOOT_
IMAGE key in the /proc/cmdline.

To create a cgroup, run the following commands in the terminal. Use
the same folders we used in the program.

mkdir -p /root/mygrp

mount -t cgroup2 none /root/mygrp

mkdir -p /root/mygrp/child

Now you can run this program:

```go
package main

import (
    "fmt"
    "os"
    "os/exec"
    "time"
    "path/filepath"
    "syscall"
    "io/ioutil"
    "strconv"
    "net"
)

func enableCgroup() {
    cgroups := "/root/mygrp"
    pids := filepath.Join(cgroups, "child")
    //os.Mkdir(filepath.Join(pids, "smj"), 0755)
```

```go
    must(ioutil.WriteFile(filepath.Join(pids, "memory.max"),
    []byte("2M"), 0700))
    // Removes the new cgroup in place after the
    container exits
    //must(ioutil.WriteFile(filepath.Join(pids, "notify_on_
    release"), []byte("1"), 0700))
    must(ioutil.WriteFile(filepath.Join(pids, "cgroup.procs"),
    []byte(strconv.Itoa(os.Getpid())), 0700))
}
func pivotRoot(newroot string) error {
    putold := filepath.Join(newroot, "/.pivot_root")
    //if err != nil {
        //return err
//    }
    // Ensure putold is removed after the function returns

    // Bind mount newroot to putold to make putold a valid
    mount point
    if err := syscall.Mount(newroot, newroot, "", syscall.MS_
    BIND|syscall.MS_REC, ""); err != nil {
    return err
}

// create putold directory
if err := os.MkdirAll(putold, 0700); err != nil{
 return err
}
    // Call pivot_root
    if err := syscall.PivotRoot(newroot, putold); err != nil {
        return err
    }

    // Change the current working directory to the new root
```

```go
    if err := os.Chdir("/"); err != nil {
        return err
    }

    // Unmount putold, which now lives at /.pivot_root
    if err := syscall.Unmount("/.pivot_root", syscall.MNT_
    DETACH); err != nil {
        return err
    }

    return nil
}

func parent() {
    cmd := exec.Command("/proc/self/exe",
    append([]string{"child"}, os.Args[2:]...)...)
    cmd.Stdin = os.Stdin
    cmd.Stdout = os.Stdout
    cmd.Stderr = os.Stderr
    cmd.Env = []string{"name=shashank"}
    cmd.SysProcAttr = &syscall.SysProcAttr{
        Cloneflags: syscall.CLONE_NEWNS |
            syscall.CLONE_NEWUTS |
            syscall.CLONE_NEWIPC |
            syscall.CLONE_NEWPID |
            syscall.CLONE_NEWNET |
            syscall.CLONE_NEWUSER,
        UidMappings: []syscall.SysProcIDMap{
            {
                ContainerID: 0,
                HostID:      os.Getuid(),
                Size:        1,
            },
        },
```

```
        GidMappings: []syscall.SysProcIDMap{
            {
                ContainerID: 0,
                HostID:      os.Getgid(),
                Size:        1,
            },
        },
    }

            must(cmd.Start())


    pid := fmt.Sprintf("%d", cmd.Process.Pid)
    fmt.Printf("obtaibed pid %s",pid)
// Code below does the following
// Creates the bridge on the host
// Creates the veth pair
// Attaches one end of veth to bridge
// Attaches the other end to the network namespace. This is
interesting
// as we now have access to the host side and the network side
until // we block.
netsetgoCmd := exec.Command("/usr/local/bin/netsetgo",
"-pid", pid)
  if err := netsetgoCmd.Run(); err != nil {
    fmt.Printf("Error running netsetgo - %s\n", err)
    os.Exit(1)
  }
  if err := cmd.Wait(); err != nil {
    fmt.Printf("Error waiting for reexec.Command - %s\n", err)
    os.Exit(1)
  }
}

}
```

```go
func child() {
    // Set the hostname for the child process
    enableCgroup()
    must(syscall.Sethostname([]byte("myhost")))

    // Now execute the command specified in the command-line
    arguments
    cmd := exec.Command(os.Args[2], os.Args[3:]...)
    cmd.Stdin = os.Stdin
    cmd.Stdout = os.Stdout
    cmd.Stderr = os.Stderr
    must(mountProc("/root/book_prep/rootfs"))
    must(syscall.Sethostname([]byte("myhost")))
if err := pivotRoot("/root/book_prep/rootfs"); err != nil{
fmt.Printf("Error running pivot_root - %s\n",err)
os.Exit(1)
}
if err := waitForNetwork(); err != nil {
                fmt.Printf("Error waiting for network -
                %s\n", err)
                os.Exit(1)
        }

    must(cmd.Run())
}

func must(err error) {
    if err != nil {
        fmt.Printf("Error - %s\n", err)
    }
}
```

```go
func main() {
    switch os.Args[1] {
    case "parent":
        parent()
    case "child":
        child()
    default:
        panic("help")
    }
}

func waitForNetwork() error {
  maxWait := time.Second * 3
    checkInterval := time.Second
    timeStarted := time.Now()
    for {
        interfaces, err := net.Interfaces()
        if err != nil {
          return err
        }
        // pretty basic check ...
        // > 1 as a lo device will already exist
        if len(interfaces) > 1 {
          return nil
        }
        if time.Since(timeStarted) > maxWait {
        return fmt.Errorf("Timeout after %s waiting for network",
        maxWait)
        }
        time.Sleep(checkInterval)
        }
}
```

```go
// this function mounts the proc filesystem within the
// new mount namespace
func mountProc(newroot string) error {
    source := "proc"
    target := filepath.Join(newroot, "/proc")
    fstype := "proc"
    flags := 0
    data := ""
//make a Mount system call to mount the proc filesystem within
the mount namespace
    os.MkdirAll(target, 0755)
    if err := syscall.Mount(
        source,
        target,
        fstype,
        uintptr(flags),
        data,
    ); err != nil {
        return err
    }
    return nil
    }

}
```

proceeding text shows the process PID added to the cgroup and the value stored in the memory.max file, which we defined in the program.

```
root@instance-1:~/mygrp# ls
cgroup.controllers        cgroup.subtree_control
cpuset.cpus.effective  io.cost.model
memory.pressure                     sys-kernel-debug.mount
cgroup.max.depth          cgroup.threads
cpuset.mems.effective  io.cost.qos
memory.stat                         sys-kernel-tracing.mount
cgroup.max.descendants  child
dev-hugepages.mount      io.pressure
proc-sys-fs-binfmt_misc.mount  system.slice
cgroup.procs                cpu.pressure
dev-mqueue.mount          io.stat
sys-fs-fuse-connections.mount  user.slice
cgroup.stat                cpu.stat                      init.scope
memory.numa_stat                    sys-kernel-config.mount
```

The proceeding text shows the process PID added to the cgroup and the value stored in the memory.max file

```
root@instance-1:~/mygrp# cd child
root@instance-1:~/mygrp/child# cat cgroup.procs
991
1018

root@instance-1:~/mygrp/child# cat memory.max
2097152
```

Summary

In the chapter, we covered the basics of how Linux containers can be created in golang.

The chapter covered the specifics of Linux containers (namespaces, cgroups, and union file systems) and how containers are realized within the Linux kernel. We wrote a Linux container and saw how, with some simple programming, we can create a simple container runtime like Docker.

You are advised to go over each exercise and try different combinations of the code. As an example, you could do the following:

1. Try a new `rootfs` rather than busybox.

2. Try container-to-container networking.

3. Experiment with more resource controls.

4. Run an HTTP server within one container and an HTTP client within another container and establish communication over HTTP.

You should now have a decent idea as to what happens under the hood within a container. Therefore, when you use different container orchestrators like Kubernetes or Swarm, you'll more easily understand what is actually happening.

CHAPTER 7

Why Choose Rust

In previous chapters you learned about virtualization in depth and how different resources like memory, CPU, and networks are virtualized both in context of VM and containers. We did a deep dive into container-based virtualization and explored with Golang-based programs how to create container sandboxes.

In this chapter we cover the basics of the Rust programming language, which allows us to build more secure container sandboxes owing to the inherent constructs of Rust programming which are more secure.

Introduction

A few years back, as a programmer struggling with constant memory bugs and erratic behavior in my code, I was desperate for a solution. That's when I stumbled upon Rust, a programming language that claimed to alleviate these issues and more. Intrigued, I decided to give it a try. To my surprise, Rust not only guaranteed memory and thread safety, but also boasted a contemporary syntax and a thriving community. Its ownership and borrowing mechanisms have enabled me to craft efficient code, free of memory leaks or data races.

Rust's package manager, Cargo, streamlines my dependency management and project building, and a plethora of community-created libraries and frameworks enable me to dive into projects without reinventing the wheel.

© Shashank Mohan Jain 2023
S. M. Jain, *Linux Containers and Virtualization*,
https://doi.org/10.1007/978-1-4842-9768-1_7

But what truly captivates me is Rust's emphasis on performance. Its zero-cost abstractions facilitate high-level programming without sacrificing performance, rivaling lower-level languages like C.

And as a programmer well versed in systems programming, I find Rust's focus on safety to be particularly well suited for an area notorious for security vulnerabilities. Rust enables me to effortlessly create secure and sturdy systems code.

I am enamored with Rust and its countless advantages. Crafting code that is not only safe and efficient but also elegant and comprehensible brings me immense joy. And with a helpful Rust community ever-ready to lend a hand and impart wisdom, I feel like I have finally found my programming home.

In the end, discovering Rust not only addressed my programming woes, but also reignited my passion for the craft. That's enough of a reason to learn this beautiful language known as Rust.

We will introduce the language in the next few pages, before we build a compelling use case like creating a Linux container with Rust.

Rust Installation

To install Rust on Ubuntu, follow these steps. These steps are specific to Ubuntu and will be different for different Distros of Linux:

1. Update the package index and install the required dependencies:

```
sudo apt update
sudo apt install curl build-essential
```

2. Download and run the Rust installation script:

```
curl --proto '=https' --tlsv1.2 -sSf https://
sh.rustup.rs | sh
```

The installation script will prompt you to proceed
with the installation. Press 1 and then press Enter to
proceed with the default installation.

3. After the installation is complete, you'll see a
    message instructing you to add the Cargo and Rust
    binaries to your PATH. Add the following line to
    your ~/.bashrc, ~/.bash_profile, or ~/.zshrc
    file, depending on which shell you use:

```
export PATH="$HOME/.cargo/bin:$PATH"
```

4. Source the updated configuration file to make the
    changes take effect in your current shell session:
    If you're using Bash:

```
source ~/.bashrc
```

If you're using Zsh:

```
source ~/.zshrc
```

5. Verify the installation by checking the version of the
    Rust compiler:

```
rustc --version
```

Variables

Similar to numerous other programming languages, Rust employs
variables. Variables serve to store data in computer memory, allowing for
its usage and manipulation throughout the program. Rust boasts unique
characteristics to bolster code safety, with variables being integral to these
features.

Variable declaration in Rust is achieved by using the `let` keyword succeeded by the variable's name and its type. For instance, to declare a variable x of type i32 (32-bit integer), we can write the following:

Note   For the code examples in this chapter, you can also try the code at the Rust Playground: `https://play.rust-lang.org/`.

```
let x: i32;
```

If we want to assign an initial value to the variable, we can do it using the equals (=) sign, like this:

```
let x: i32 = 42;
```

Rust also offers *type inference*, which means that, in many cases, you don't have to explicitly specify the type. The compiler can infer the type based on the value assigned:

```
let x = 42; // x is inferred to be of type i32
```

It is crucial to understand that Rust variables are, by default, immutable, meaning their values cannot be altered once assigned:

```
let x = 42;
```

Then we cannot assign a new value to x like this:

```
x = 24; // This will result in a compile-time error
```

However, we can make a variable mutable by using the `mut` keyword, like this:

```
let mut x = 42;
x = 24; // This will work fine
```

The following is an example of variable declaration in Rust:

```rust
fn main() {
    let x: i32 = 42; // Declare an immutable variable x of
                        type i32
    let mut y = 24; // Declare a mutable variable y with
                        initial value 24
    y = 12; // Assign a new value to y

    let z = x + y; // Declare a new variable z that is the sum
                        of x and y

    println!("x = {}", x); // Print the value of x
    println!("y = {}", y); // Print the value of y
    println!("z = {}", z); // Print the value of z
}
```

Its output is as follows:

```
x = 42
y = 12
z = 54
```

In the prior example, we declare an immutable variable x of type i32 and a mutable variable y with an initial value of 24. We then assign a new value 12 to y. Next, we declare a new variable z that is the sum of x and y. Finally, we print the values of x, y, and z.

The following is another example of variable declaration in Rust:

```rust
fn main() {
    let x = 42; // Declare a variable x of type i32 (type is
                    inferred)
    let mut y = x; // Declare a mutable variable y with initial
                    value of x
    y = 12; // Assign a new value to y
```

```
    println!("x = {}", x); // Print the value of x
    println!("y = {}", y); // Print the value of y
}
```

Output:

```
x = 42
y = 12
```

In this example, we declare a variable x with an initial value of 42. We then declare a mutable variable y with the initial value of x. We assign a new value of 12 to y.

Data Types

Rust has several built-in data types that allow developers to store, manipulate, and access data in different ways. Understanding the different data types is a fundamental aspect of Rust programming.

Primitive Data Types

Rust has the following primitive data types:

- **Bool**: Bool is a primitive type in Rust that represents a boolean value. It can have two possible values, true or false. For example:

  ```
  let is_rust_awesome: bool = true;
  ```

- **Char**: Char is a primitive type in Rust that represents a single Unicode scalar value. It is denoted by single quotes, ' '. For example:

  ```
  let letter: char = 'A';
  ```

- **Integer**: Rust offers four separate integer types, having both signed and unsigned versions. The types include i8, i16, i32, i64, and their corresponding unsigned counterparts u8, u16, u32, and u64. The signed integers employ the i prefix, while unsigned integers use the u prefix, as shown in the following examples. The size and range of these integer types differ accordingly.

```
let a: i32 = 42;
let b: u8 = 255;
```

- **Floating-point**: Rust has two different floating-point types, f32 and f64, as shown in the following examples. They represent single- and double-precision floating-point values, respectively.

```
let x: f32 = 3.14159;
let y: f64 = 2.71828;
```

- **Unit type**: Unit type is a special type in Rust that has only one possible value, (). It is used when a function does not return anything or when we need to represent a void value. In the following example, the greet() function doesn't return any value; it just prints a message. Calling greet() and assigning its return value to result assigns the unit type () to result.

```
fn greet() {
    println!("Hello, Shashank!");
}

fn main() {
    let result: () = greet();
}
```

Compound Data Types

Rust also has compound data types that can be used to group values of different types into a single type. The two main compound data types in Rust are tuples and arrays:

- **Tuple**: A tuple is a collection of values of different types. Tuples are declared using parentheses, ( ). For example:

```
let person: (&str, i32) = ("Alice", 32);
```

- **Array**: An array is a fixed-size collection of values of the same type. Arrays are declared using square brackets, [ ]. For example:

```
let numbers: [i32; 5] = [1, 2, 3, 4, 5];
```

Apart from the built-in data types, Rust enables developers to fashion custom data types employing structs, enums, and unions. These data types facilitate the construction of intricate data structures that depict real-world entities.

Structs, enums, and unions constitute three composite data types in Rust, which permit the bundling of data and the creation of novel types with distinct attributes compared to built-in types. In the following sections, we'll delve into each of these data types and examine examples to clarify their application.

Structs

In Rust, structs are a fundamental data type that enables the grouping of related data and the creation of new types with distinct characteristics from the built-in types. For instance, we can define a basic struct as follows:

```
struct Rectangle {
    width: u32,
    height: u32,
}
```

In this example, we've defined a struct called Rectangle that has two fields: width and height. The width and height fields are both of type u32, which is an unsigned 32-bit integer. We can use this struct to represent a rectangle with a given width and height.

We can create instances of the Rectangle struct like this:

```
let rect = Rectangle { width: 30, height: 50 };
```

This creates a new Rectangle instance with a width of 30 and a height of 50.

We can access the fields of a struct using dot notation like this:

```
println!("The area of the rectangle is {} square pixels.",
rect.width * rect.height);
```

This will print The area of the rectangle is 1500 square pixels. to the console.

The following is the complete code:

```
struct Rectangle {
    width: u32,
    height: u32,
}

fn main() {
    let rect = Rectangle { width: 30, height: 50 };
    println!(
        "The area of the rectangle is {} square pixels.",
        rect.width * rect.height
    );
}
```

Enums

Enums are another fundamental data type in Rust. They allow us to define a type that can have one of several variants. Here's an example of a simple enum:

```rust
enum Fruit {
    Apple,
    Banana,
    Orange(String),
    Mango { ripeness: u8 },
}
```

In this example, we have an enum called `Fruit` that can represent different types of fruit. The first two variants, `Apple` and `Banana`, have no associated values. The third variant, `Orange`, takes a `String` parameter to represent the variety of the orange. This allows us to differentiate between different types of oranges, like `"navel"` oranges and `"blood"` oranges. The fourth variant, `Mango`, is a bit more complex. It takes a named parameter, `ripeness`, which is a `u8` value representing how ripe the mango is. This allows us to represent different degrees of ripeness, from unripe to fully ripe.

The following enum can be used to represent a variety of different fruits and their associated characteristics, showcasing how enums in Rust can be used to create flexible and powerful data types.

```rust
let my_fruit = Fruit::Orange(String::from("navel"));
```

In this example, we're creating a variable called `my_fruit` using the `Fruit` enum. We're using the `Orange` variant, and passing in the `String` value `"navel"` to represent the variety of the orange.

This variable could be used later on in the program to represent the fruit we're working with, allowing us to handle different types of fruit using a single enum type. For example, we could write a function that takes a `Fruit` parameter and performs different actions based on the variant of the enum.

We can use a `match` expression to handle the different variants of the `Fruit` enum as follows. Don't worry about the `match` part for now. We will cover it in later sections in the context of loops and conditions.

```
match my_fruit {
    Fruit::Apple => println!("This is an apple!"),
    Fruit::Banana => println!("This is a banana!"),
    Fruit::Orange(variety) => println!("This is an orange of
    the {} variety!", variety),
    Fruit::Mango { ripeness } => println!("This is a mango that
    is {}% ripe!", ripeness),
}
```

Following is the complete code for showing how matching expressions work with enums:

```
enum Fruit {
    Apple,
    Banana,
    Orange(String),
    Mango { ripeness: u8 },
}

fn main() {
    let my_fruit = Fruit::Orange(String::from("navel"));

    match my_fruit {
        Fruit::Apple => println!("This is an apple!"),
        Fruit::Banana => println!("This is a banana!"),
        Fruit::Orange(variety) => println!("This is an orange
        of the {} variety!", variety),
        Fruit::Mango { ripeness } => println!("This is a mango
        that is {}% ripe!", ripeness),
    }
}
```

In this example, we're using a `match` statement to perform different actions based on the variant of the `Fruit` enum stored in the `my_fruit` variable. If `my_fruit` contains the `Apple` variant, we print `"This is an apple!"` to the console. If it contains the `Banana` variant, we print `"This is a banana!"`. If it contains the `Orange` variant, we extract the associated `String` value using a variable `variety` and use it to print `"This is an orange of the {variety} variety!"`. Finally, if it contains the `Mango` variant, we extract the associated `u8` value using a named parameter `ripeness` and use it to print `"This is a mango that is {ripeness}% ripe!"`.

Using a `match` statement with an enum allows us to handle different cases in a clean and concise way, making our code more readable and easier to maintain.

Unions

Unions are similar to structs in that they allow us to group related data together. However, unions have a different set of properties. Specifically, they allow us to define a type that can hold one of several different types of data, but only one at a time. Here's an example of a simple union:

```
union IntOrFloat {
    i: i32,
    f: f32,
}
```

In this example, we've defined a union called `IntOrFloat` that can hold either an `i32` or an `f32`, but not both at the same time. We can use this union to represent a value that could be either an integer or a floating-point number.

We can create instances of the `IntOrFloat` union like this:

```
let value = IntOrFloat { f: 3.14 };
```

This creates a new IntOrFloat instance with the f field set to 3.14.

Unions are another way to combine different types of data under a single type. However, unlike structs and enums, unions can only hold one value at a time. The size of the union is determined by the largest member. This makes a union useful in situations where you need to store different types of data in the same space.

Here's an example of a union:

```rust
union Data {
    num: i32,
    ptr: *const i32,
}

fn main() {
    let mut data = Data { num: 42 };
    unsafe {
        println!("data.num = {}", data.num);
        data.ptr = &data.num as *const i32;
        println!("data.ptr = {:?}", data.ptr);
    }
}
```

The following output of the prior program shows the functioning of unions:

```
data.num = 42
data.ptr = 0x7ffc403337d0
```

In this example, we define a union called Data that can hold either an i32 or a pointer to an i32. We then create an instance of the union and initialize it with the value 42. We then use the unsafe keyword to assign the address of the num field to the ptr field, and print out both fields.

Note   Rust's data types provide a powerful and flexible way to represent complex data structures in your code. Understanding how to use them effectively is key to writing high-quality Rust programs.

Functions

Functions are a fundamental building block of Rust programs. They allow you to group together a set of instructions that can be executed repeatedly and, potentially, with different arguments. In this section, we'll explore Rust's functions in more detail, including how to define them, pass arguments, and return values.

Defining Functions

Functions in Rust are defined using the fn keyword, followed by the function name, and then a set of parentheses that may include zero or more arguments. Here's an example:

```
fn greet(name: &str) {
    println!("Hello, {}!", name);
}
```

In this example, we define a function called greet that takes a single argument of type &str (a string slice) and prints out a greeting message using that argument. The function does not return a value.

Calling Functions

Once you've defined a function, you can call it from other parts of your code using the function name followed by a set of parentheses containing any arguments. Here's an example:

```rust
fn main() {
    greet("Isha");
    greet("Shashank");
}
```

In this example, we call the greet function twice with different names. When the program is run, it will print out two greeting messages, one for each name.

Function Arguments

Functions in Rust can take zero or more arguments, which are defined within the parentheses following the function name. Arguments can be of any valid Rust data type, including custom structs and enums. Here's an example:

```rust
struct Book {
    title: String,
    author: String,
    year: u32,
}

fn print_book(book: &Book) {
    println!("'{}' by {} ({})", book.title, book.author,
    book.year);
}
```

```
fn main() {
    let beginning = Book {
        title: "Beginning of Infinity".to_string(),
        author: "David Deutche".to_string(),
        year: 2011,
    };

    print_book(&beginning);
}
```

In this example, we have a Book struct that contains fields for the title, author, and year of publication. We also have a function called print_book that takes a reference to a Book struct and prints out the title, author, and year in a formatted string.

In main(), we create a Book instance called beginning, and pass a reference to it to the print_book function. The function then prints out the book's title, author, and year using the formatted string.

Using a struct like Book allows us to group related data together and pass it around as a single entity. We can then define functions that operate on this data in a clean and organized way, making our code more modular and easier to read.

Function Return Values

Functions in Rust can also return values using the -> syntax followed by the return type. Here's an example:

```
fn square(x: i32) -> i32 {
    x * x
}
fn main() {
    let result = square(4);
    println!("4 squared is {}", result);
}
```

In this example, we define a function called `square` that takes a single `i32` argument and returns the square of that argument. The `main` function calls the `square` function with an argument of 4, and then prints out the result.

Function Scope and Lifetime

Variables defined within a function have a scope that is limited to that function. They are created when the function is called, and destroyed when the function returns. This means that they cannot be accessed from other parts of your code. Here's an example:

```
fn main() {
    let x = 42;
    {
        let y = 13;
        println!("x = {}, y = {}", x, y);
    }
    // y is not in scope here
    println!("x = {}", x);
}
```

In this example, we define a variable x within the `main` function, and then define another variable y within a block scope. When the program is run, it will print out the values of x and y within the block scope, and then print out the value of x again outside of the block scope.

Function Overloading

As far as Rust as a programming language is concerned, function overloading is not supported, unlike in programming languages such as C++, as the Rust language designers decided to use generics as an alternative.

Generics

The use of generics is a flexible means to write functions and data structures that work with any type, not just specific ones. Using type parameters by enclosing them in angle brackets (<>) after the name of the function allows the function to operate with any type. For example:

```
fn max<T>(a: T, b: T) -> T
where T: std::cmp::PartialOrd
{
    if a > b {
        a
    } else {
        b
    }
}
```

In this example, the max function takes two parameters of the same type T and returns a value of type T. The where clause specifies that T must implement the PartialOrd trait, which is required for comparing values with >. The PartialOrd trait is a Rust standard library trait that defines the partial_cmp method for comparing values. For now don't worry about traits, as we will cover them in the last section of this chapter.

You can also use generics with structs and enums to define data structures that can hold any type. For example:

```
struct Pair<T> {
    first: T,
    second: T,
}
```

```
enum Option<T> {
    None,
    Some(T),
}
```

In these examples, `Pair` and `Option` are parameterized by type T, so they can hold values of any type.

In conclusion, Rust allows you to write functions that work with different types using generics. This allows you to write more reusable code that can work with any type that implements the required traits. Rust does not support function overloading, but the use of generics provides a more flexible alternative.

Conditional Logic

In Rust, there are several ways to implement conditions and control flow, including if/else statements, loops, and match expressions.

If/Else Statements

If/else statements are used to implement simple conditions in Rust. These statements evaluate a condition and perform specific actions depending on whether the condition is true or false.

Here is an example:

```
fn main() {
    let num = 10;

    if num < 5 {
        println!("The number is less than 5.");
    } else {
        println!("The number is greater than or equal to 5.");
    }
}
```

In this example, the program checks if the value of num is less than 5. If it is, it prints "The number is less than 5." Otherwise (else), it prints "The number is greater than or equal to 5."

Loops

Loops are used to execute a block of code repeatedly until a specific condition is met. In Rust, there are three types of loops: loop, while, and for. As an example:

```
fn main() {
    let mut counter = 0;

    loop {
        counter += 1;

        if counter == 10 {
            break;
        }
    }

    println!("The counter is {}", counter);
}
```

In this example, the program initializes a variable counter to 0 and then enters an infinite loop using the loop keyword. Inside the loop, the program increments the value of counter by 1 and checks if it equals 10. If it does, the loop is exited with a break statement.

The while keyword is used to create a loop that executes as long as a specific condition is true. Here's an example:

```
fn main() {
    let mut counter = 0;

    while counter < 10 {
```

```
        counter += 1;
    }

    println!("The counter is {}", counter);
}
```

In this example, the program initializes a variable counter to 0 and then enters a while loop that continues to execute as long as the value of counter is less than 10. Inside the loop, the program increments the value of counter by 1.

The for keyword is used to iterate over a range or collection of values. Here's an example:

```
fn main() {
    for i in 0..10 {
        println!("The value of i is {}", i);
    }
}
```

Match Expressions

Match expressions are used to compare a value against a set of patterns and perform different actions based on which pattern matches. In Rust, match expressions are a powerful tool for implementing complex conditions and control flow. Here's an example:

```
fn main() {
let number = 6;
match number {
    0 => println!("Number is zero"),
    1 | 2 => println!("Number is one or two"),
    3..=5 => println!("Number is between three and five"),
    _ => println!("Number is greater than five"),
}
}
```

In this example, the match statement is used to compare the value of the number variable against different patterns. The patterns are listed after the match keyword and are separated by =>.

The first pattern matches when number is equal to 0 and prints "Number is zero". The second pattern matches when number is equal to 1 or 2 and prints "Number is one or two". The third pattern matches when number is between 3 and 5 (inclusive) and prints "Number is between three and five". The _ pattern is a catch-all pattern that matches anything not previously matched, and prints "Number is greater than five" in this case.

The ..= operator is used to create an inclusive range in Rust. In this example, it is used to match any number between 3 and 5, inclusive.

The match statement is a powerful tool in Rust that can be used to handle different cases and patterns in a concise and readable way. It is often used in Rust programs for error handling, as well as for pattern matching in functional programming.

Exception Handling

In Rust, error handling is based on the concept of Result and the panic! macro.

The Result type in Rust is used to represent either a successful value or an error. It is defined as follows:

```
enum Result<T, E> {
    Ok(T),
    Err(E),
}
```

Here, T represents the type of the successful value, while E represents the type of the error. The Ok variant holds the successful value, while the Err variant holds the error value.

When a function can potentially fail, it should return a Result type. The caller of the function can then handle the result using pattern matching, as shown in the following example:

```
use std::fs::File;
use std::io::Read;

fn read_file(filename: &str) -> Result<String,
std::io::Error> {
    let mut file = File::open(filename)?;

    let mut contents = String::new();
    file.read_to_string(&mut contents)?;

    Ok(contents)
}

fn main() {
    match read_file("example.txt") {
        Ok(contents) => println!("File contents: {}",
        contents),
        Err(err) => println!("Error reading file: {}", err),
    }
}
```

In this example, we have a function called read_file that attempts to open a file, read its contents into a string, and return the string as a Result. If any of these operations fail, the corresponding std::io::Error is returned as an Err value. In the main function, we use a match expression to handle the Result, printing the file contents if the operation was successful or the error message if it failed.

Rust does not have traditional exception handling like many other programming languages, but it does have a feature called panic! that can be used to abort the program and print an error message. Here's an example:

```rust
fn divide(a: i32, b: i32) -> i32 {
    if b == 0 {
        panic!("Attempt to divide by zero");
    }

    a / b
}

fn main() {
    let result = divide(10, 2);
    println!("10 / 2 = {}", result);

    divide(10, 0);
}
```

This example should result in the following output:

```
Finished dev [unoptimized + debuginfo] target(s) in 0.98s
    Running `target/debug/playground`
thread 'main' panicked at 'Attempt to divide by zero', src/
main.rs:3:9
note: run with `RUST_BACKTRACE=1` environment variable to
display a backtrace
```

In this example, we have a function called divide that attempts to divide two integers and return the result. If the second argument is 0, we use panic! to abort the program and print an error message. In the main function, we call divide twice: once with valid arguments and once with an invalid argument. The first call succeeds and prints the result, but the second call fails and causes the program to abort.

While panic! is not a traditional exception-handling mechanism, it can be used in situations where an unrecoverable error has occurred and the program cannot continue. Rust also provides a catch_unwind function that can be used to catch panics in library code, but this is generally not recommended for application-level error handling.

Rust Security Features

Rust, a systems programming language, was initially unveiled by Mozilla in 2010. Its primary objective is to deliver memory safety while preserving optimal performance. As a language, Rust is designed to be safe, concurrent, and speedy. Additionally, it is a strongly typed language, which implies that each value in Rust possesses a fixed type that remains unaltered during runtime.

A key aspect of Rust is its unique ownership system, specifically designed to avoid typical errors like null pointer exceptions and data races. In Rust, each value has a designated owner who has exclusive access to it. When the owner goes out of scope, the value gets dropped, consequently freeing its memory. Additionally, the ownership system incorporates the concept of borrowing, which permits multiple references to a value to coexist simultaneously, provided that only one of these references is mutable.

Lifetimes are another essential aspect of Rust, serving as a mechanism to monitor relationships between value references. In Rust, every reference possesses a lifetime that dictates the duration of its validity. By checking lifetimes during compile time, the Rust compiler aids in avoiding frequent errors like dangling pointers.

Rust encompasses a variety of features that contribute to its power and expressiveness, such as pattern matching, closures, and traits. Pattern matching enables developers to compare values against specific patterns, simplifying the handling of distinct cases. Closures represent functions capable of capturing variables from their surrounding scope for later use. Traits, akin to interfaces in other languages, allow developers to specify a collection of methods that a type must implement.

Rust is a modern and sturdy programming language that is great for creating secure software. It prioritizes safety and speed, which makes it very popular among developers working on complex code. Additionally, Rust has a clear and flexible language structure with many advanced features, which makes it an attractive choice for system programmers to use to create compelling applications.

Ownership System

In Rust, variables function similarly to how ownership works when selling say a book to a friend. The person to whom you sell the book possesses it and can use it however they please. In the same way in Rust, when a value is assigned to a variable, the variable becomes the owner of the value. If the variable is then passed to a function or assigned to another variable, the ownership is transferred to the new variable, and the old one no longer has ownership. This feature allows Rust to manage memory precisely, which can improve code efficiency and help prevent bugs.

Rust's ownership system is a fundamental feature aimed at preventing prevalent programming mistakes, such as null pointer exceptions and data races. Within Rust, each value is assigned an owner who has exclusive access to it. As the owner goes out of scope, the value gets dropped, subsequently releasing its memory. This method guarantees that values remain valid and that no unforeseen interactions occur between various sections of the program.

The ownership system in Rust encompasses borrowing, a feature that permits the coexistence of multiple references to a single value, provided that only one reference is mutable. In the book example this would be more like lending the book, where you can take the ownership back. This enables developers to craft code that is both secure and efficient. For instance, creating numerous read-only references to the same value allows for sharing the data without copying it. This approach proves especially beneficial when working with sizable data structures.

The following in an example of moving a value from one variable to another:

```
let mut s1 = String::from("shashank");
let s2 = s1;
// Here, ownership of the string "shashank" is moved from
`s1` to `s2`
```

Returning ownership from a function works as follows:

```
fn create_vector() -> Vec<i32> {
    let v = vec![1, 2, 3, 4, 5];
    v // Return ownership of the vector to the caller
}

fn main() {
    let my_vector = create_vector();
    println!("my_vector: {:?}", my_vector);
}
```

This code example features a function called create_vector(), which generates a vector comprising five integers. The function passes ownership of the vector to the caller by using the variable v, which is moved automatically out of the function and into the variable my_vector.

As a result of the function call, my_vector is now in possession of the vector's ownership. We can utilize my_vector to access and modify the data within the vector.

This example highlights how Rust's ownership system enables the transfer of value ownership between functions, ensuring that each value has only one owner at any given point. It also demonstrates how Rust's built-in data structures, such as vectors, work in unison with ownership to efficiently manage memory.

Lifetimes

To draw a comparison with real life, imagine you're hosting a party and you want to ensure that there is enough food for everyone. You contract a caterer to supply food for the duration of the event. However, the caterer needs to know when the party will end to make sure that they bring enough food for the whole event. This is similar to how *lifetimes* work in Rust. They specify how long a borrowed value will be used so that Rust can manage memory correctly.

For instance, if a function returns a reference to a variable, Rust needs to know that the reference will not be utilized after the variable goes out of scope, to prevent the reference from being utilized after the variable has been deallocated.

Lifetimes in Rust are a technique for tracking the connections between references to values. Each reference has a lifetime in Rust, indicating how long the reference is valid. The Rust compiler validates lifetimes during compile time, which helps avoid typical errors such as dangling pointers. Lifetimes can be indicated using syntax such as 'a or 'b, and they are employed to ensure that references do not exist beyond the lifespan of the values they refer to.

Lifetimes are especially crucial when working with mutable references in Rust. Only one mutable reference can exist to a specific value at a time, which prevents data races that occur when multiple threads try to modify the same data concurrently. By enforcing strict guidelines surrounding mutable references, Rust guarantees that programs are both safe and efficient.

The following is an example of using a reference with a shorter lifetime:

```rust
fn print_first_word(s: &str) {
    let first_word = s.split_whitespace().next().unwrap();
    println!("{}", first_word);
}

fn main() {
    let my_string = String::from("hello shashank");
    print_first_word(&my_string[..5]); // Pass a reference to
    the first 5 characters of the string
}
```

Here's an example of using a reference with a longer lifetime:

```rust
fn get_longest<'a>(x: &'a str, y: &'a str) -> &'a str {
    if x.len() > y.len() {
        x
```

```rust
    } else {
        y
    }
}
fn main() {
    let s1 = "hello";
    let s2 = "shashank";
    let result = get_longest(s1, s2);
    println!("The longest string is: {}", result);
}
```

In this example, s1 represents a string literal with the value "hello", while s2 is another string literal containing the value "shashank". The get_ longest function is subsequently called using these two string references as arguments, with the outcome assigned to the variable result.

The get_longest function evaluates the lengths of both input strings and returns a reference to the lengthier string. As "shashank" is longer than "hello" in this instance, the function provides a reference to the string "shashank", which is then allocated to the variable result.

Pattern Matching

Picture yourself playing "Guess Who?" with a friend. In this game, both players have a set of cards featuring various characters, and they take turns asking yes-or-no questions to deduce the other's character. For instance, asking "Does your character wear glasses?" allows you to eliminate characters without glasses if your friend answers affirmatively. This resembles Rust's *pattern matching* concept, where values are tested against specific patterns, leading to different actions based on the outcomes. Rust's pattern matching is commonly employed to destructure complex types like enums or structs, facilitating easier access to their fields or variants. It also aids in writing concise and clear code when handling diverse cases or error conditions.

In Rust, pattern matching is a robust feature that empowers developers to compare values against distinct patterns, enabling the management of various cases in a program. For instance, pattern matching can address errors or process different kinds of input data.

Rust's pattern matching is especially potent due to its capacity to destructure values, allowing for the extraction of values from intricate data structures like tuples or enums. Furthermore, pattern matching can be utilized to match ranges, boolean values, and other primitive types.

The following is an example of matching on an enum variant:

```rust
enum Animal {
    Cat,
    Dog,
    Rabbit,
    Bird,
}

fn main() {
    let pets = vec![
        Animal::Cat,
        Animal::Dog,
        Animal::Rabbit,
        Animal::Bird,
        Animal::Cat,
        Animal::Dog,
        Animal::Rabbit,
        Animal::Bird,
    ];

    for pet in pets {
        match pet {
            Animal::Cat => println!("You have a cat as a pet!"),
```

```
        Animal::Dog => println!("You have a dog as a pet!"),
        Animal::Rabbit => println!("You have a rabbit
        as a pet!"),
        Animal::Bird => println!("You have a bird as a pet!"),
    }
  }
}
```

This code defines an enumeration (enum) called Animal with four variants: Cat, Dog, Rabbit, and Bird. Each variant represents a different type of animal. In the main() function, a vector called pets is created and populated with instances of the Animal enum. The vector contains two instances of each animal variant: Cat, Dog, Rabbit, and Bird. The code then enters a for loop that iterates over each element in the pets vector. The match expression is used to match each variant of the Animal enum and perform a specific action based on the matched variant. For each pet in pets, the match expression checks the variant and executes the corresponding code block. It prints a message indicating the type of animal the pet represents. The output will be something like this:

```
You have a cat as a pet!
You have a dog as a pet!
You have a rabbit as a pet!
You have a bird as a pet!
You have a cat as a pet!
You have a dog as a pet!
You have a rabbit as a pet!
You have a bird as a pet!
```

The following is an example of matching on a range:

```rust
fn main() {
    let num = 5;
    match num {
        1..=3 => println!("Small"),
        4..=6 => println!("Medium"),
        _ => println!("Large"),
    }
}
```

This code demonstrates the usage of the match expression with range patterns to categorize a number into different size categories.

In the main() function, a variable num is assigned the value 5. The match expression is used to compare the value of num against different range patterns. Each pattern is separated by => and followed by an associated code block. The first pattern, 1..=3, represents a range from 1 to 3 (inclusive). If the value of num falls within this range, the corresponding code block println!("Small") will be executed. The second pattern, 4..=6, represents a range from 4 to 6 (inclusive). If the value of num falls within this range, the code block println!("Medium") will be executed. The underscore (_) acts as a wildcard pattern and matches any value that did not match the previous patterns. In this case, if the value of num does not fall within the ranges specified in the previous patterns, the code block println!("Large") will be executed.

Since the value of num is 5, it falls within the range of 4..=6, and therefore the code block println!("Medium") will be executed.

Closures

Picture yourself as a teacher tasked with grading students' homework. Each student has unique homework, yet you must apply the same grading criteria to all homework. One method involves writing the grading criteria on a whiteboard and having students grade their work using those criteria. This is analogous to a *closure* in Rust—a code block that can be defined once and reused with varying input values. Rust closures are functions that capture variables from their surrounding environment, which can be stored in variables or passed as arguments to other functions. Closures are beneficial for creating adaptable code for different situations or inputs.

Closures enable the creation of concise and expressive code by capturing variables from their enclosing scope for later use. They are particularly helpful when working with iterators, a crucial feature in Rust.

Iterators in Rust are lazily evaluated, meaning values are generated only as needed. This approach is often more efficient than generating all values simultaneously. Closures are used to define operations that should be performed on each value generated by an iterator.

The following is an example of defining a closure and using it with map:

```
fn main() {
    let numbers = vec![1, 2, 3, 4, 5];
    let squares = numbers.iter().map(|x| x * x);
    for sq in squares {
    println!("{}", sq);
    }

}
```

Capturing a variable from the enclosing scope can be achieved like this:

```
fn main() {
    let name = "Shashank";
    let greet = || println!("Hello, {}!", name);
    greet();

}
```

Traits

Picture yourself searching for a new car with specific requirements—it must be fast, reliable, and fuel-efficient. These criteria are comparable to "traits" as they outline the desired characteristics in a car. While car shopping, you can compare models based on how well they meet your requirements. Similarly, in Rust, *traits* define a collection of behaviors or features a type must possess. Traits enable you to write generic code that works with any type exhibiting those behaviors or features, just as you can compare any car that satisfies your requirements.

Like interfaces in other languages, traits allow developers to specify a set of methods that a type must implement. This facilitates writing generic code compatible with various types. Traits can be employed to define shared functionality, such as serialization or comparison.

Traits prove particularly valuable when working with generics in Rust. Generics empower developers to create code compatible with multiple data types. Traits are used to outline the available operations on those types, ensuring the code is both safe and efficient.

In the example below, we will demonstrate how to use Traits in Rust:

```
// Define a trait for any object in the game
trait GameObject {
    fn update(&mut self);
}

trait Renderable {
    fn render(&self);
}

struct Player {
    x: f32,
    y: f32,
}
```

```rust
impl GameObject for Player {
    fn update(&mut self) {
        self.x += 1.0;
        self.y += 1.0;
    }
}

impl Renderable for Player {
    fn render(&self) {
        println!("Rendering player at ({}, {})", self.x, self.y);
    }
}

struct Enemy {
    x: f32,
    y: f32,
}

impl GameObject for Enemy {
    fn update(&mut self) {
        self.x -= 1.0;
        self.y -= 1.0;
    }
}

impl Renderable for Enemy {
    fn render(&self) {
        println!("Rendering enemy at ({}, {})", self.x, self.y);
    }
}
```

```
fn main() {
    let mut player = Player { x: 0.0, y: 0.0 };
    let mut enemy = Enemy { x: 10.0, y: 10.0 };

    player.update();
    player.render();

    enemy.update();
    enemy.render();
}
```

In this example, we establish a GameObject trait representing any object within the game and a Renderable trait representing objects that can be displayed on the screen. We then define two structs: Player and Enemy, implementing the GameObject and Renderable traits for each.

Within the main function, we instantiate both Player and Enemy structs, calling the update and render methods for each.

This example illustrates how traits can be employed in Rust to outline shared behavior for distinct object types and how structs can implement multiple traits to define their behavior in various contexts. In this case, we utilize the GameObject trait to describe common behavior for in-game objects and the Renderable trait to specify behavior for objects that can be rendered onscreen.

Summary

In this chapter we looked at the basics of Rust programming to get a feel of what the language brings to the table. We covered various aspects related to different programming constructs and covered advanced features related to the security aspects advocated by Rust. In Chapter 8 we will visit the Linux namespaces and related concepts needed to create a Linux container in Rust.

CHAPTER 8

Containers in Rust

In Chapter 7 we looked at basic Rust programming constructs and identified what makes Rust a secure language. We also examined in detail various Rust structures that can be used to accomplish safe programming. In this chapter we explore how to use Rust to create Linux containers and sandboxes. We will mainly focus on the concept of namespaces under Rust and how to use them for process isolation.

Refreshing Linux Namespaces?

Linux namespaces are like a superpower for the Linux kernel. They give processes their own secret hideouts where they can do their thing without anyone else snooping around. It's like having separate little worlds within the big Linux universe. These worlds have their own stuff (resources) like network interfaces, IDs, and even file systems, so no one steps on each other's toes. It's like having multiple parties going on at the same time without any drama or fights breaking out. People who work with Linux love using namespaces because they make life so much easier. It's a clever way to keep resources within linux processes more organized and prevent chaos from taking over.

Here is a brief review of some of the namespaces we will be using in this chapter to create a Linux container in Rust:

- **PID**: Isolates the process ID number space.

- **Network**: Provides a separate network stack for each namespace.

© Shashank Mohan Jain 2023
S. M. Jain, *Linux Containers and Virtualization*,
https://doi.org/10.1007/978-1-4842-9768-1_8

- **Mount**: Allows each namespace to have its own set of file system mounts.

In Rust, the Nix library (`https://crates.io/crates/nix`) provides a way to create and manage Linux namespaces.

1. Install Rust in the Linux VM: `https://www.rust-lang.org/tools/install`. I use Ubuntu as the operating system, so all examples given in this chapter work on Ubuntu.

2. Install dependencies to get started:

   ```
   sudo apt-get install build-essential
   ```

Creating a PID Namespace

This section describes how to create a PID namespace using Rust.

First create a new project by using the following command:

```
cargo new <<project name>>
```

Then change directory to into the project root using `cd <<project name>>`. The directory structure looks like this

```
my_project_name/
├── src/
│    └── main.rs
└── Cargo.toml
```

Since this project uses the Nix library, create a `Cargo.toml` file in the root directory with the following content:

```
[dependencies]
nix = "0.22.1"
```

Now edit `main.rs` and add the following code:

```
use nix::sched::{clone, CloneFlags};
use nix::sys::signal::{self, Signal};
use nix::unistd::{execvp, ForkResult};
use std::ffi::CString;
use std::slice;

// Function to be executed in the child process
fn child_function() -> isize {
    // Check if we are in the new PID namespace
    if nix::unistd::getpid() == nix::unistd::Pid::from_raw(1) {
        println!("We are in the new PID namespace!");
    } else {
        println!("We are still in the old PID namespace.");
    }

    // Return a value indicating the child process's
    exit status
    // You can change this value as per your requirement
    0
}
```

```rust
fn main() {
    // Define the stack size for the child process
    let stack_size = 1024 * 1024; // 1MB stack size for the
    child process

    // Allocate memory for the child process stack
    let mut child_stack = vec![0; stack_size];

    // Define the flags for the clone system call
    let flags = CloneFlags::CLONE_NEWPID;

    // Execute the clone system call to create a new process
    match unsafe {
        // Obtain a mutable pointer to the child stack
        let child_stack_ptr = child_stack.as_mut_ptr();
        // Create a slice from the child stack pointer and the
        stack size
        let child_stack_slice = slice::from_raw_parts_
        mut(child_stack_ptr, stack_size);

        // Call the clone system call with the child function,
        // child stack, flags, and None for the closure argument
        clone(
            Box::new(child_function),
            child_stack_slice,
            flags,
            None,
        )
    } {
        Ok(child_pid) => {
            // Check if we are in the parent or child process
            if child_pid == nix::unistd::Pid::from_raw(0) {
                // Parent process
```

```
    // Wait for the child process to terminate
    match nix::sys::wait::waitpid(child_
    pid, None) {
        Ok(_) => println!("Child process
        terminated"),
        Err(err) => eprintln!("Failed to wait for
        child process: {:?}", err),
    }
} else {
    // Child process

    // Set up signal handling for SIGCHLD
    unsafe {
        signal::signal(Signal::SIGCHLD,
        signal::SigHandler::SigIgn)
            .expect("Failed to set SIGCHLD
            handler");
    }

    // Execute a new program in the new PID
    namespace
    let program = CString::new("/bin/sh").unwrap();
    let args = [
        CString::new("/bin/sh").unwrap(),
        CString::new("-c").unwrap(),
        CString::new("echo Hello from the new PID
        namespace").unwrap(),
    ];

    // Execute the specified program with the given
    arguments
    execvp(&program, &args).expect("Failed to
    execute program");
```

```
        }
    }
    Err(err) => eprintln!("Failed to create new process:
    {:?}", err),
  }
}
```

The preceding code utilizes the Nix library to accomplish two tasks: create a new PID namespace and execute a program within that namespace.

The child_function() is a function that will be executed specifically in the child process. Its purpose is to determine whether the process is in the new or old PID namespace and print an appropriate message accordingly.

In the main function we start by defining the size of the stack that will be allocated for the child process. Next we create a buffer to hold the stack of the child process, and then we set the flags for creating a new PID namespace.

Next we invoke the clone() function to create a new process. It takes as arguments the child_function to be executed in the child process, the buffer representing the child process stack, the flags for creating a new PID namespace, and additional options (none in this case).

If the clone function call is successful, the return value contains the process ID of the child process. We use this information to determine if we are in the parent or child process.

If we are in the parent process, we wait for the child process to terminate using the waitpid function from the Nix library and print a message accordingly. If we are in the child process, we set up the handling of the SIGCHLD signal to ignore it. This is accomplished using the signal function from the Nix library.

Finally, we execute a new program within the new PID namespace using the execvp function from the Nix library. We specify the program to be executed ("/bin/sh") and any command-line arguments as an array. In this case, we execute a shell command to print Hello from the new PID namespace.

The code combines various Nix library functions and Rust language features to achieve the goal of creating a new PID namespace and executing a program within it, demonstrating the functionality and capabilities of namespace isolation.

Build and execute the program using the following commands:

```
cargo build
cargo run
```

Creating a Network Namespace

This section presents an example of how to create a new network namespace in Rust. The following code demonstrates how to create a new network namespace and verify its isolation by inspecting the network configuration using the ip a command.

```
use nix::sched::{clone, CloneFlags};
use nix::sys::wait::{waitpid, WaitPidFlag};
use nix::unistd::{execvp, ForkResult};
use std::ffi::CString;
use std::process::Command;

// Function to be executed in the child process
fn child_function() -> isize {
    // Validate network configuration within the new network
    namespace
    let output = Command::new("ip")
        .arg("a")
```

```
        .output()
        .expect("Failed to execute command");

    // Print the network configuration within the new network
    namespace
    println!("Network configuration within the new network
    namespace:\n{}", String::from_utf8_lossy(&output.stdout));

    0
}

fn main() {
    // Define the stack size for the child process
    let stack_size = 1024 * 1024; // 1MB stack size for the
    child process

    // Allocate memory for the child process stack
    let mut child_stack = vec![0; stack_size];

    // Define the flags for the clone system call
    let flags = CloneFlags::CLONE_NEWNET;

    // Execute the clone system call to create a new process
    match unsafe {
        // Obtain a mutable pointer to the child stack
        let child_stack_ptr = child_stack.as_mut_ptr();
        // Create a slice from the child stack pointer and the
        stack size
        let child_stack_slice = std::slice::from_raw_parts_
        mut(child_stack_ptr, stack_size);

        // Call the clone system call with the child function,
        child stack, flags, and None for the closure argument
        clone(
            Box::new(child_function),
```

```
            child_stack_slice,
            flags,
            None,
        )
    } {
        Ok(child_pid) => {
            // Check if we are in the parent or child process
            if child_pid == nix::unistd::Pid::from_raw(0) {
                // Parent process

                // Wait for the child process to terminate
                waitpid(child_pid, Some(WaitPidFlag::empty())).
                expect("Failed to wait for child process");
                println!("Child process terminated");
            } else {
                // Child process

                // Specify the program and arguments to execute
                within the new network namespace
                let program = CString::new("/bin/sh").unwrap();
                let args = [
                    CString::new("/bin/sh").unwrap(),
                    CString::new("-c").unwrap(),
                    CString::new("echo Hello from the new
                    network namespace").unwrap(),
                ];

                // Execute the specified program with the given
                arguments
                execvp(&program, &args).expect("Failed to
                execute program");
            }
        }
```

```
        Err(err) => eprintln!("Failed to create new process:
        {:?}", err),
    }
}
```

In the code we define the size of the stack for the child process and create a buffer for the stack.

The CloneFlags::CLONE_NEWNET flag is set to indicate that we want to create a new network namespace.

We use the clone function to clone the current process, specifying the child function, stack, flags, and options. This creates a child process in a new network namespace.

If we are in the parent process, we wait for the child process to terminate and print a message indicating the termination.

If we are in the child process, we use the execvp function to replace the current process with a new program execution. In this case, we execute the shell command echo "Hello from the new network namespace".

Within the child process, we execute the ip a command using the Command struct from the std::process module. This command retrieves the network configuration within the new network namespace.

The output of the ip a command is captured and printed, displaying the network configuration within the new network namespace.

Running the preceding code produces the following network configuration output, which confirms that the code successfully created a new network namespace. It shows that the loopback interface (lo) is present in the namespace, but it is currently inactive (state DOWN). This is expected as the loopback interface is typically brought up by the operating system or network configuration tools.

By inspecting the network configuration output, we can verify that the new network namespace is isolated from the host network namespace.

```
root@instance-1:/home/jain_sm/pid-namespace-test# Network
configuration within the new network namespace:
1: lo: <LOOPBACK> mtu 65536 qdisc noop state DOWN group default
qlen 1000
    link/loopback 00:00:00:00:00:00 brd 00:00:00:00:00:00
```

In the provided network configuration output, we can see that there is a loopback interface (lo) present in the namespace. The state DOWN indicates that the loopback interface is currently inactive. This is expected since the interface is typically brought up by the operating system or network configuration tools.

Creating a Mount Namespace

In Unix and Linux operating systems, there is a unique approach to handling file systems compared to Windows. Instead of having separate drives like C: and D:, Unix and Linux adopt a single directory hierarchy starting from the root directory (/). To make a file system accessible, it needs to be attached, or "mounted," to a specific directory within this hierarchy. For instance, when you connect a USB drive to your computer, the system may automatically mount the file system on the USB drive to a directory such as /media/usb. Consequently, any files present on the USB drive become accessible under that directory.

On the other hand, a mount namespace represents a feature provided by the Linux kernel that enables individual processes to possess their own distinct perspective of the system's mount points. This isolation capability allows different processes to observe diverse sets of files at the same path within the file system. Mount namespaces play a crucial role in the functioning of containers. When a process operates within a container, it obtains its dedicated mount namespace, ensuring that it remains isolated from the rest of the system's files.

Here is an example of how to create a new mount namespace in Rust:

```rust
extern crate nix;
extern crate libc;

use nix::mount::{mount, umount2, MsFlags, MntFlags};
use nix::sched::{unshare, CloneFlags};
use nix::sys::stat::Mode;
use nix::unistd::{execvp,chdir,ForkResult, chroot};
use nix::NixPath;
use std::ffi::CString;
use std::os::unix::prelude::AsRawFd;
use std::os::unix::io::FromRawFd;
use std::fs;
use std::os::unix::fs::symlink;

fn main() {
    match unsafe { unshare(CloneFlags::CLONE_NEWNS |
    CloneFlags::CLONE_NEWPID) } {
        Ok(_) => {
            // Create a new directory to be used as the
            new root
            fs::create_dir_all("/tmp/newroot").expect("Failed
            to create /tmp/newroot directory");

            // Make the mounts in the new mount
            namespace private
            mount(
                None::<&str>,
                "/",
                None::<&str>,
                MsFlags::MS_PRIVATE | MsFlags::MS_REC,
                None::<&str>,
            )
```

```rust
        .expect("Failed to make mounts private");

        // Mount the /proc file system as private within
        the new mount namespace
        mount::<str, str, str, str>(
            Some("proc"),
            "/proc",
            Some("proc"),
            MsFlags::MS_PRIVATE,
            None::<&str>,
        )
        .expect("Failed to mount /proc");

        // Set the new root as the current root
        chroot("/").expect("Failed to change root");

        // Validate mounted file systems within the new
        mount namespace
        let program = CString::new("/bin/sh").unwrap();
        let args = [
            CString::new("/bin/sh").unwrap(),
            CString::new("-c").unwrap(),
            CString::new("mount -l").unwrap(),
        ];

        // Execute the specified program with the given
        arguments
        execvp(&program, &args).expect("Failed to execute
        program");
    }
    Err(err) => eprintln!("Failed to create new process:
    {:?}", err),
    }
}
```

In the preceding code, we do a few things.

We use unshare, which creates a new mount namespace. Next we use bind mount to mount the root directory of host to some path on root.

This will copy all the rootfs mounts to this place. For this code I am not doing it and using the host root itself.

Then mount the /proc at /proc.

Then you can chroot into that directory.

From there you can launch the program/shell into the namespace.

Writing Complete Container Code

Here is the complete container code, which creates all three namespaces and gives us a shell within the isolated environment we created:

```
extern crate nix;
extern crate libc;

use nix::mount::{mount,  MsFlags};
use nix::sched::{clone, unshare, CloneFlags};
use nix::sys::wait::{waitpid, WaitPidFlag};
use nix::unistd::{execvp, chroot};
use nix::sys::signal::{self, Signal};
use std::ffi::CString;
use std::os::unix::prelude::AsRawFd;
//use std::os::unix::io::FromRawFd;
use std::fs;
//use std::os::unix::fs::symlink;
use std::process;

fn network_namespace() {
    // Create a new network namespace
    match unsafe { unshare(CloneFlags::CLONE_NEWNET) } {
        Ok(_) => {
```

```rust
            // Perform network-related configuration within the
            new network namespace

            println!("We are in the new network namespace!");
        }
        Err(err) => eprintln!("Failed to create new network
        namespace: {:?}", err),
    }
}

fn pid_namespace() {
    // Create a new PID namespace
    match unsafe { unshare(CloneFlags::CLONE_NEWPID) } {
        Ok(_) => {
            // Perform PID-related configuration within the new
            PID namespace

            println!("We are in the new PID namespace!");
        }
        Err(err) => eprintln!("Failed to create new PID
        namespace: {:?}", err),
    }
}

fn mount_namespace() {
    // Create a new mount namespace
    match unsafe { unshare(CloneFlags::CLONE_NEWNS) } {
        Ok(_) => {
            // Create a new directory to be used as the
            new root
            fs::create_dir_all("/tmp/newroot").expect("Failed
            to create /tmp/newroot directory");
```

```rust
            // Make the mounts in the new mount
            namespace private
            mount(
                None::<&str>,
                "/",
                None::<&str>,
                MsFlags::MS_PRIVATE | MsFlags::MS_REC,
                None::<&str>,
            )
            .expect("Failed to make mounts private");

            // Mount the /proc file system as private within
            the new mount namespace
            mount::<str, str, str, str>(
                Some("proc"),
                "/proc",
                Some("proc"),
                MsFlags::MS_PRIVATE,
                None::<&str>,
            )
            .expect("Failed to mount /proc");

            // Set the new root as the current root
            chroot("/").expect("Failed to change root");

            println!("We are in the new mount namespace!");
        }
        Err(err) => eprintln!("Failed to create new mount
        namespace: {:?}", err),
    }
}

fn child_function() -> isize {
```

```rust
    network_namespace();
    pid_namespace();
    mount_namespace();

    // Execute an interactive shell within the namespace
    let program = CString::new("/bin/sh").unwrap();
    let args = [
        CString::new("/bin/sh").unwrap(),
    ];

    execvp(&program, &args).expect("Failed to execute
    program");

    // The execvp call replaces the current process, so this
    line should not be reached
    println!("Execvp failed!");

    // Exit the child process
    process::exit(1);
}

fn main() {
    let stack_size = 1024 * 1024; // 1MB stack size for the
    child process
    let mut child_stack = vec![0; stack_size];

    let flags = CloneFlags::CLONE_NEWNET | CloneFlags::CLONE_
    NEWPID | CloneFlags::CLONE_NEWNS;

    match unsafe {
        let child_stack_ptr = child_stack.as_mut_ptr();
        let child_stack_slice = std::slice::from_raw_parts_
        mut(child_stack_ptr, stack_size);
```

```
        clone(
            Box::new(child_function),
            child_stack_slice,
            flags,
            None,
        )
    } {
        Ok(child_pid) => {
            if child_pid == nix::unistd::Pid::from_raw(0) {
                // Parent process
                waitpid(child_pid, Some(WaitPidFlag::empty())).
                expect("Failed to wait for child process");
                println!("Child process terminated");
            } else {
                // Child process
                // Set up signal handling for SIGCHLD
                unsafe {
                    signal::signal(Signal::SIGCHLD,
                    signal::SigHandler::SigIgn)
                        .expect("Failed to set SIGCHLD
                        handler");
                }
            }
        }
        Err(err) => eprintln!("Failed to create new process:
        {:?}", err),
    }
}
```

Here is what you will see as output:

```
root@instance-1:/home/jain_sm/pid-namespace-test# We are in the
new network namespace!
We are in the new PID namespace!
We are in the new mount namespace!
```

The following list summarizes the role of each of the functions in the preceding code:

- network_namespace(): This function creates a brand-new environment just for networking resource. In this special space, network interfaces, IP addresses, and routing tables are kept separate from the rest of the system. It's like having a secret network club where only certain processes can hang out. To make this happen, the function uses the unshare() function with a special flag called CloneFlags::CLONE_NEWNET.

- pid_namespace(): This function creates the PID namespace, a unique playground for processes. Inside this space, each process gets its very own set of PIDs. It's like giving each process its own special ID card that only works within that namespace. To make this magic happen, the function also uses the unshare() function, but this time with the CloneFlags::CLONE_NEWPID flag.

- mount_namespace(): This function creates a whole new world for file systems. It's like having a separate universe where you can mount and unmount file systems without affecting the rest of the system. To make this happen, the function uses the unshare() function again, but this time with the CloneFlags::CLONE_NEWNS flag. It does some extra tricks, like creating a new root directory and isolating the mounts from the rest of the system. It even mounts the /proc file system specifically for process-related information.

- child_function(): This function is where the real action starts. It is like the VIP entrance to the namespaces party. It calls the network_namespace(), pid_namespace(), and mount_namespace() functions to set up the desired namespaces. Then, it throws an interactive shell using the execvp() function. This basically swaps the child process with a fancy shell process, so you can have a chat with it inside the created namespaces. How cool is that?

- main(): The big boss of the program, this function prepares the stage for the child process and sets the flags for the desired namespaces. Using the clone() function, it creates a new child process. If it's the parent process which is running then, it waits patiently for the child to finish its thing. Once the child is done, it prints a message saying so. On the other hand, if it's the child process, it's all about setting up some special handling for signals by the parent process and then diving right into the child_function().

Summary

In this chapter we looked at how to create isolated sandboxes in Rust using examples of a PID namespace, network namespace, and mount namespace. Building upon the knowledge of what these namespaces are, we gave explored how to create these namespaces in Rust as well as how to create a small container using them.

Index

A

address_space, 85
Alternative virtualization
    mechanisms
    Docker, 26
    hotplug capability, 31
    novm, 29, 30
    POSIX interface, 26
    project dune, 28, 29
    unikernels, 27, 28, 30
    WebAssembly, 31
Application binary interface
    (ABI), 3

B

Back-end drivers, 12, 20
Bind mount, 36
Block devices, 83, 85
Block I/O cgroup
    bio structure, 65
    bio_vec, 66
    purpose, 63
    request, 65
    request flows, user space to
        device, 64
    request_queue, 64
Branches, 90

Buffer heads, 86
bytecode, 2

C

CFQ group, 68, 71
cgroup.controllers, 49
cgroup.events, 50
cgroup.procs, 50
Cgroups
    and cap, 134
    cgroup controllers, 48
    CPU (*see* CPU cgroups)
    creation, 48–51, 136
    fairness, 68–71
    GRUB_CMDLINE_LINUX_
        DEFAULT, 135
    memory.max file, 142
    mygrp, 48, 49
    PID, 135, 142
    system reboots, 135
    throttling, 71–80
    version v1 and v2, 48
cgroup.subtree_control, 50
child() function, 133
child_function(), 200
clone flags, 100
clone() function, 200

© Shashank Mohan Jain 2023
S. M. Jain, *Linux Containers and Virtualization*,
https://doi.org/10.1007/978-1-4842-9768-1

CLONE_NEWNS flag, 199
Cloudflare, 32
cmd.Wait(), 130
Code privilege level (CPL), 8
Complete container code, 194–200
Compound data types
   application, 152
   array, 152
   tuples, 152
Conditional logic
   break statement, 164
   for keyword, 165
   If/else statements, 163
   loops, 164
   while keyword, 164
Container-based virtualization, 3–4
Container framework
   cgroups, 134–143
   Golang install, 97
   Mount Proc FS, 116–119
   namespaces, 98–107
   network namespaces, 119–134
   root FS, 110–116
   unshare, 95
   UTS namespace, 95, 96
   shell program, 107–110
ContainerID, 104
Container layer, 92
Container's IP, 130, 131
Control groups, *see* Cgroups
CPU cgroups
   block I/O, 63–66
   cff_bandwith_used function, 60
   cfs_bandwidth, 59

CPU resource control,
   types, 52, 53
curr member, 58
delta_exec, 56
group scheduling, 57
I/O tasks, 56
Pick_next_entity, 59
sched_entities, 58, 59
schedulers, 52
task_struct structure, 55
types, 53
update_curr function, 55
vruntime, 53, 56, 59
CPU virtualization
   binary translation, 9
   CPL, 8
   paravirtualization, 9, 10
   protection rings, 8

D

Dentry, 36, 84, 85
Device model, 4, 5
Dune architecture, 28, 29

E

Enums, 154
   Apple and Banana, 154
   Mango, 154
   match expression, 155
   matching expressions, 155
   match statement, 156
   Orange, 154

String value, 156
ESX, 2
eventfd, 13
    edge-triggered system, 24
    epoll_wait, 24
    ioeventfd, 24, 25
    I/O thread, 25
    IPC, 24
    irqfd, 25
    network packet flow, 23
    vs. Linux pipe, 25
    OOM, 25
Excessive trapping, 17
Extended Page Table (EPT), 7, 13

F

Fairness, 68–71
Fastly, 32
File descriptor (FDs), 13, 20,
    23–25, 84, 86
File system (FS)
    layered, 89
    mountProc, 116–119
    OverlayFS, 90–93
    primer, 83–87
    procfs, 87
    pseudo, 87–89
    union, 90
    VFS, 84
firstap, 121
Front-end drivers, 12, 20
FS primer
    address_space, 85

block device, 85
buffer heads, 86
except direct I/O, 85
Ext4, 87
fdatasync(fd), 86
file descriptor, 86
file maps into page
    cache, 85
fsync(fd), 86
layers under kernel, 87
Linux abstracts, 84
in Linux act, 83
ProcFS, 87
sync(), 86
vfsmount data structure, 85
write call, 86
Full virtualization, 9, 11
Functions, 158
    arguments, 159
    calling, 159
    defining, 158
    greet, 159
    overloading, 161
    print_book, 160
    return values, 160
    scope, 161

G

Generics, 162
    angle brackets, 162
    Pair and Option, 163
    PartialOrd trait, 162
    structs, 162

GidMappings, 104
Go, 96
Golang installation, 97
GSX, 2
Guests, 2, 3

H

Hardware-assisted
    virtualization, 10
Host, 3
Hotplug capability, 31
hotplug-dimm module, 31
Hypercall, 10
Hypervisors, 2, 89
    device model, 5
    software, 4
    VMM, 4, 5

I

Inode, 84
Instruction set
    architecture (ISA), 3
Intel Vt-x instruction set, 15–18
Interprocess communication
    (IPC), 24, 37, 45, 98, 118
ioeventfd, 25
I/O memory management unit, 13
IO virtualization
    full virtualization, 11
    modes, 11
    paravirtualization, 11, 12
IPC namespace, 37

J

Java programs, 2

K

Kernel Virtual Machine (KVM),
    15, 19, 21–23, 27
KSM (kernel same page merging), 89
KVM kernel module, 22, 23

L

Layered FS, 89
Linux containers, 33, 38, 144
Linux namespaces, 33, 38, 98,
    107, 180–182

M

match statement, 156, 166
Match expressions, 165–166
memory.events, 51
Memory management unit
    (MMU), 6, 13
memory.max file, 142
Memory virtualization
    EPT, 7
    guest OS, 6
    memory abstractions, 6
    shadow page tables, 7
Mount namespace, 191, 194
mountProc FS, 116–119
mountProc() function, 132
Multiple read layers, 92

must() function, 119, 133
mygrp, 49
mytap1, 120
mytap2, 120
myuts binary, 99
myuts.go, 99

N

Namespaces, 33, 48, 122–128
   add device, 45
   and set up, 106
   cgroups, 37, 98
   clone flags, 100, 102
   container, 101
   controls, 34
   function parent, 106
   GidMappings, 104
   Golang process, 100
   hostname, 106
   I/O streams, 100
   isolation, 34
   IPC, 37, 98
   Linux kernel, 34, 98
   mount, 35–36, 98, 106, 182
   myuts binary, 99
   myuts.go, 99
   network, 37, 98, 181
   non-root, 104
   PID, 35, 98
   pivot root, 106
   process ID number, 181
   /proc/self/exe, 106
   time, 38–44

UidMappings, 104
user space–based
   applications, 34
UTS, 35, 98, 100, 106
veth pairs, 105
netsetgo, 128, 129
netsetgoCmd command, 133
Network namespace, 37, 40, 44,
   122, 187
   clone function, 190
   CLONE_NEWNET flag, 190
   configuration, 188
   virtual networking, 119–134
Nix library, 182, 183, 187
Non-block devices, 83
Non-trapping instructions, 17
novm, 29, 32
nsproxy structure, 39, 40

O

Out of memory (OOM), 25, 51
OverlayFS
   base layer, 91
   diff directory, 92
   diff layer, 91
   directory, 91
   Docker driver device
     mapper, 93
   Linux Kernel, 90
   multiple read layers, 92
   OverlayFS v1, 90
   OverlayFS v2, 91
   unmount, 92

P

Paravirtualization, 9, 10
    back-end drivers, 12
    eventfd, 13
    vs. full virtualization, 11
    network packet flow, 13
    SRIOV, 14
    virtqueue, 12
parent() function, 133
pdflush, 86
PID namespace, 35, 182, 186, 199
pivot_root, 110
pivotRoot() function, 119, 132
Pivot root, 106
Primitive data types
    bool, 150
    char, 150
    floating-point, 151
    integer, 151
    unit type, 151
proc mount, 116
procfs FS, 87
Project Dune, 28
Protection rings, 8
Pseudo FS, 87–89

Q

Quick Emulator (QEMU), 15
    guest, 20
    hypervisor, 19
    I/O, 20, 31
    KVM kernel module, 19, 31
    packet flow, 21

    virtio-blk, 20
    virtio-net, 20
    virtqueues, 20

R

Read-only FS, 89
Rectangle struct, 153
Root file system, 119
rootfs, 93
Root FS, 110–116
Rootless containers, 105
Rust, 145
    advantages, 146
    Animal enum, 175
    closures, 177
    configuration, 147
    create_vector(), 171
    data types, 150
        compound, 152
        primitive, 150
    emphasis on performance, 146
    enums, 154
    error handling, 166
    exception handling, 167
    functions, 158
    GameObject trait, 180
    get_longest function, 173
    guarantees, 172
    installation, 146, 147
    lifetimes, 172
    Linux container, 146
    main() function, 176
    match expressions, 165

mount namespace, 192
ownership, 170
package manager, 145
panic, 167
pattern matching, 173, 174
read_file, 167
security reatures
    memory safety, 169
    ownership system, 169
    software, 169
    value references, 169
structs, 152
traits, 178
unions, 156
update and render methods, 180
variable, 148–150, 170
Rust's ownership system, 171

S

secondtap, 121
Service tree, 68
Shadow page tables, 7
Shell program, 107–110
Single root I/O virtualization
    (SRIOV), 14
std::process module, 190
Structs, 152
Superblock, 84

T

tap devices, 23, 25, 119–121
tap interfaces, 121

task_struct data structure, 38
testns namespace, 45
Throttling, 71–80
Time namespace, 38–44
tun and tap, 119
tun device, 119

U

UidMappings, 104
Unikernels, 3, 26–28
Union FS, 90
Unions
    Data, 157
    IntOrFloat, 156
Unix and Linux operating
    systems, 191
unshare() function, 199
Utility function, 119
UTS namespace, 95, 96, 106, 109

V

veth pairs, 105, 121, 128
vfsmount, 35, 36, 85
Vhost based data
    communication, 22, 23
Virtio, 12
Virtqueue, 12, 13, 20, 23, 31
Virtual file system (VFS), 64, 84, 85
    dentry, 84
    file, 84
    inode, 84
    superblock, 84

Virtualization
    abstraction, 2
    container-based approach, 3
    CPU, 8–10
    guests, 2
    history, 1, 2
    hypervisors, 2, 4 (*see also*
        Hypervisors)
    intermediary code, 2
    I/O, 11–14
    memory, 6–8
    process-level, 2
    techniques, 2
    unikernels, 3
    VM-based approach, 3
Virtual machine (VM), 2–4, 16
Virtual machine extensions (VMX)
    root mode, 10
Virtual machine monitor (VMM),
    4–10, 17, 18, 26–30
Virtual networking
    child() function, 133
    cmd.Start(), 128
    cmd.Wait(), 128, 130
    container's IP, 130, 131
    container's namespace, 122
    host IP address, 131
    host's namespace, 121, 122
    mountProc() function, 132

    must() function, 133
    netsetgo, 128, 129
    netsetgoCmd command, 133
    network interfaces, 120
    network namespace, 122–128
    IP packets, 119
    parent/child process, 132
    parent() function, 133
    pivotRoot() function, 132
    tap interfaces, 121
    tun and tap devices, 119–121
    veth pairs, 121, 128
    VMs, 119
    waitForNetwork() function, 132
VM-based provisioning, 89
VM-based
    virtualization, 3, 8, 33
VM control structure
    (VMCS), 10, 22
VM Entries, 10, 18
VM Exits, 10, 18
VMware, 2
vruntime, 53, 55, 56, 59

W, X, Y, Z

waitForNetwork() function, 132
waitpid function, 186
WebAssembly, 31

Printed in the United States
by Baker & Taylor Publisher Services